Praise for The Nurturing Leader

"The Nurturing Leader is an excellent guide for both the seasoned and developing leaders as it provides practical tools for skill development and strategies. I find it very useful in my new role as Minister of Information and Communications."
Peter Both
Minister of Information and Communications
Government of Upper Nile State, South Sudan

"Gives leadership teams the important questions to ask on an ongoing basis to support systemic growth and facilitate change when required. An easy read that is very comprehensive in terms of the strategies and tools it provides!"
Dr. Lucy Miller
Chief Superintendent, Calgary Catholic School District

"A practical and accessible guide to the nuts 'n bolts of organizational life. This is a handy reference that every leader can benefit from."
Doyle Peterson
Vice-President, Summer Institute of Linguistics International

"This comprehensive guide is of great benefit to community leaders who want to grow from grassroots efforts to a thriving organization with well-managed programs that address local needs."
Debra M. Armstrong
Executive Director, LINKages Society

"Insightful, with concise tools providing breadth and depth needed for an organization to grow and to succeed. This will help management or executives to produce fruitful results."
Francois Robert,
President, Global PartnerLink

"The Nurturing Leader' is an easy, step-by-step tool for leaders to help them manage organizational change."
Holly Davidson
National Events Manager, UNICEF Canada

The Nurturing Leader

A Toolkit for Every Season of Organizational Growth

authorHOUSE®

AuthorHouse™
1663 Liberty Drive
Bloomington, IN 47403
www.authorhouse.com
Phone: 1-800-839-8640

Published by AuthorHouse   05/18/2012

ISBN: 978-1-4772-0842-7 (sc)
ISBN: 978-1-4772-0843-4 (e)

Acknowledgements:

We wish to thank all those who nurtured us, and without whom we could not have completed this book: the Locke family -- Laura, Jesse, Marki, Meghan and Peter for their editing prowess, humour, inspiration, endless patience, espresso and prayers; Mavis Christie for her nurturing support and foresight in preparing and packing food for us when we ventured to Africa to test the concepts contained in our book; Daphne Willems for her innovative design and perseverance with our GANTT charts and ever-changing amendments; Andy Nichols for his resourceful photography; François Robert and Global PartnerLink, without whose support this book would not have begun. Last but not least we would like to express our deepest appreciation to the many sources of wisdom, inspiration, technique and strategy sprinkled throughout this book.

Table of Contents

Acknowledgements

Prologue   i

Introduction: Why Leaders Need Help   ii
A Tall Order   iii
Capacity Building   v
Another Perspective On Organizations   v
The Nurturing Leader   vii
The Garden   viii

About this book   ix
How to Use This Book   ix
Structure of this Book   ix
Elements and Tools   x

Section One - Welcome to the Garden   1

Chapter One: Organization as Garden   2
Systems   3
Tending to the Garden   4
Weedy Problems and Overall Signs of Trouble   5

Chapter Two: The Importance of Values   6
Stage One – Identify Values   7
Stage Two – Define Purpose   9
Stage Three – Clarify Decision-Making   9
Stage Four – Develop a Work Plan   10

Chapter Three: Organizational Capacity   11
Eight Key Ingredients   12
Capacity Building – Defined   14

Chapter Four: From Need to Action   **15**
Assessing Organizational Capacity – HR Focus   16
How Organizations Function   18
Management Tools   18
Systems-Systems-Systems   19

Chapter Five: Alignment and Misalignment   **20**
Organizational Tiers   21

Chapter Six: Managerial Tools Grid   **23**
Assessing Alignment   25
How Systems Can Contribute to Misalignment   26

Section Two - Role of the Consultant   **27**

Chapter Seven: The Third Party Point-of-View   **28**
Perspective - More than Sight   30
Experts vs Advisers   32
Key Roles   33

Chapter Eight:
Relationship Between Consultant & Leader   **34**
Agreeing to Work Together   36
Stages of Relationship   39
Job description(s)   40
Group Facilitator   41
Business Architect Consultant   41
Organization Design Consultant   42
Johari Window   44

Chapter Nine: Team Approach   **45**

Section Three - Seasons of the Garden   **48**

Chapter Ten: Winter: Initiation & Assessment
Reflection **50**
High Level Assessment 51
Startup 52
Relationship Cycle 53

Chapter Eleven: Assessment: Looking at the Plot and
Surrounding Area **55**
Environmental Scan 56
Strategic Questions for Strategic Leaders 57
Historical Highs and Lows 59
SWOT Analysis 60
Discernment 62
Ask Staff 62

Chapter Twelve: Envisioning & Strategic Planning **64**
Strategic Planning Process: Sample 65
The Visioning Process - Dark Star/ Bright Star 67
Slogan 70
Mind Map 70

Chapter Thirteen: Spring: Preparing to Act and Getting
Buy-in **72**
Sustaining Change Equation 73
Big Picture 73
Buy-In 74
Skills and Tools 75
Manage Risks 75
Action 76
Lasting Change 76

Chapter Fourteen: Staging the Process **80**
Situation Analysis 81
Describe Your Situation 81
Program Logic Model (Sample) 82
Implementation Readiness - Action Work Plan 83
Reality Check #1 – Session Rating Scale 85

Chapter Fifteen: Leadership	**86**
Leadership Attributes Analysis Tool	87
Strategic Leadership Attributes Test	88
Operational Leadership Attributes Test	89
Team Leadership Attributes Test	90
Chapter Sixteen: Facilitating Growth	
Tactics & Techniques	**91**
How to Brainstorm	92
Everybody has a Great Idea	93
Distillation Exercise	93
De Bono Gets it Right Again: Six Thinking Hats	94
Chapter Seventeen: Summer:	
Putting the Plan into Action	**95**
Intro: Teach the Team to Act	96
Managing Change and Growth - Project Charter	97
Management Plan	97
Work Breakdown	97
Work Breakdown Structure	98
Critical Path	98
Progress Plan	99
GANTT Chart	100
Teaching/coaching/mentoring	101
Systems Review and Improvement	101
Capacity Assessment – Sample	102
Financial Management – Budget Variances	104
Goal Attainment Scale	105
Chapter Eighteen: Fall: Harvest and Celebration	**107**
Outcomes and Evaluation	108
How to Conduct a Focus Group	109
Checklist for Planning and Benefiting from Focus Group	111
Time to Contemplate	112
Performance Appraisal	112
Communication	113
Celebration	113

Chapter Nineteen: Next: Back to Winter   **114**
Winter – Start Over   115
Reflection and Evaluation   115

Epilogue   **117**

Contact Us   **117**

Bibliography   **117**

Appendix: Other Resources and Tools   **118**
Consulting and Capacity Building   118
Non-Profit and Community Organizations   120
Tools – Consulting, Business, Legal, etc.   121
Workshop Ideas   123
Organizational Theory:
Change Management and Community Development   124
Policy   125

About the Authors   **126**

The Nurturing Leader and Purpose of this Book

This is a practical guide for organizational leaders to help them fulfill the mandate of their organizations in an organic fashion. Life being what it is, organizations are continually under pressure in big and small ways. They can lose their focus; they can drift from their mandates; they can become stuck in old ways of thinking as the world around them changes dramatically. Leaders must adapt by aligning and realigning their vision, mission and objectives on an ongoing basis using an organic approach.

This guide uses the analogy of tending to a growing garden. Every culture on earth can relate to this metaphor, especially people in remote parts of the earth. Like a garden, organizations need tending as they grow through the seasons.

Organizational leaders and managers are like gardeners who need tools for addressing issues and change in their organizations. They need to identify and exercise their unique gifts in a variety of situations, in conjunction with others.

How does one person facilitate change? There is no standard process. In fact, it can be complex, frustrating and confusing. The leader may have to adopt a variety of approaches - some planned, structured and explicit; others more organic, unfolding and implicit.

This guide will share ideas, thoughts and experience, providing leaders with valuable tools and links to other resources.

Introduction: Why Leaders Need Help

The world in which organizations exist is constantly changing. Organizational strategies and processes that worked at one time may slowly become ineffective or inefficient in a new evolving environment and leaders may not know that something is adrift. And if they know it, they may be unsure what has gone wrong, why, and how best to respond.

It is the leader's responsibility to continually provide the right kinds of change. Some are very skilled at this, while others struggle and fail. Even the best often need help from others on the outside to identify the issues and help them adjust.

"It is the leader's responsibility to continually provide the right kinds of change."

A Tall Order

Organizational leaders achieve results through others. Leadership, then, requires vision, self-mastery, action, and a nurturing attitude – which in turn requires humility, great planning, spontaneity, management skills, and courage. That's a tall order for any one person!

Leadership theory makes for great books and study. Applying all of these principles and living them out is quite another story. The reality can be much harder than expected — an executive role is very demanding. Within a short time, many leaders can find themselves overwhelmed or frustrated. Organizations, with challenging mandates, diverse personnel and interconnected functions, structures and operations, can be very complex.

In fact, organizations can be full of contradictions. By definition, they are driven by missions motivated by core beliefs or values. For example, a social justice organization seeks to help the poor. To accomplish such a daunting task requires good governance and an effective strategic plan, pursued by specialized personnel and executed in a coordinated fashion. But if it is to succeed, that organization cannot override its mandate – it cannot place its structure, staff, plans and processes above the people it is there to serve.

Many organizations find themselves in fundamental conflicts, hindering them from living out their values with integrity. This is particularly true of not-for-profit, human service organizations and government departments, as well as the for-profit sector. After years of attempting great things for their clients, these organizations can find themselves in need. Lacking key resources, they often turn inward, focusing on their own issues, becoming isolated from stakeholders. With time, they can be like an overgrown garden, out-of-control or mired in weeds.

Leaders may not know which specific issues they need to address, and this may create uncertainty within the organization. They may struggle with efficiency, effectiveness or accountability — focusing on their own needs rather than those they exist to serve. Often, they may take an ineffective approach, run out of money, and not know what to do. Or perhaps worse, they settle for mediocrity, continuing on despite doing little good.

Many leaders often perceive the organization's internal challenges. The organization itself may have a reluctant corporate culture, complex bureaucratic policies and procedures, staff and financial shortages, miscommunication, elusive stakeholders and uncaring societies.

Externally, the challenges may be even worse. It's difficult championing a cause in some environments even if everyone agrees on the end goals. Organizations sometimes have lofty goals set in troubling contexts with long-term struggles, such as homelessness or terrorism. As passionate as they may be, few leaders have the combination of gifts, entrepreneurial spirit, connections, resources and experience to pull everyone together to accomplish their organization's goals. This can reduce their capacity to effectively and efficiently address their mandate.

"Leaders are like gardeners who need tools for addressing issues and change in their organizations."

Capacity Building

If successful, capacity building addresses these issues head-on. It develops leaders and develops their organizations. It points them in the right direction, shows them how to go forward, and brings them closer to their goals, ultimately fulfilling their cause. When done in the right spirit, with the right goals and the right people, it can address many daunting challenges. It cultivates and equips leaders. It addresses strategic questions inside and outside organizations. Ultimately, it will align the organization's mandate, plan, people and processes.

Another Perspective on Organizations

Organizations are abstract entities, and are hard to get a grip on. It may be helpful to look at organizations in a fresh way.

"We are leaving the age of organized organizations and moving into an era where the ability to understand, facilitate, and encourage processes of self-organization will become a key competence. It's impossible to develop new styles of organization and management while continuing to think in old ways."
                    Gareth Morgan

Peter Senge, author of *The Fifth Discipline: The Art and Practice of The Learning Organization*, suggests that organizations must continually adapt if they are to thrive and survive. One of his main principles is the value of decentralizing leadership in organizations to enhance everyone's productivity. Senge argues that organizations must build capacity at all levels to succeed.

Like a garden, each section of the organization needs to be growing and producing results in a way that adds to the overall envisioned harvest.

People are made of flesh and blood; they find themselves subject to psychological, social, political, and economic forces. An organization cannot simply be built, powered, harnessed and fixed like a machine.

> *"An organization has no presence beyond that of the people who bring it to life."* Gareth Morgan

Rather than seeing organizations as one realm, like an assembly line, set of relationships or reification of values, the new thinking is that organizations involve a network connecting all of these realms. To fulfill capacity requires development and alignment of people, parts and processes.

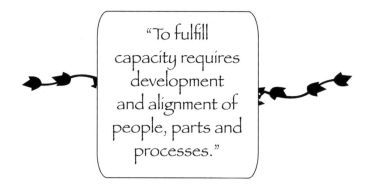

"To fulfill capacity requires development and alignment of people, parts and processes."

The

Nurturing Leader

Rather than leading in all areas, nurturing leaders empower others to lead. They stand by their employees and managers - listening and learning as well as guiding.

The nurturing leader is also a great teacher - a trainer. This type of leader is a facilitator, asking key questions to help sort out the team's priorities and thinking things through. Above all, leaders should be advisors, giving cues when asked and needed.

Nurturing leaders equip others to fulfill their mandates. That way, leadership can be multiplied. In order to do that, the leader at times may have to stand back and remain in some ways a third party.

This is perhaps the most powerful secret to being a great leader. Standing by the employees, a leader can help them identify issues as they relate to the organization's mission and vision. This creates the synergy and space that employees need to address their particular issues and reach their full potential.

The Garden

What this book does is use a metaphor — the garden — to get at the workings of these complex entities. In the past, theorists looked at organizations in a mechanistic fashion, as if they function like a factory full of machines. From this perspective, organizations can be engineered. This is very useful for breaking down tasks for some business purposes, but it may ignore critical elements.

An organization, since it is made up of living beings, is alive. In other words, an organization is like a garden.

A garden is a living thing, growing and bearing fruit. Similarly, an organization is a living entity of a certain character, generating outcomes through its people.

The organization's "plants" are people with different talents, who can display certain attributes and harvest different kinds of outcomes. At the same time, a garden is very complex, with many factors that will affect its life and fruits. **The leader of the organization has many living things to contend with on an ongoing basis.** Sometimes the organization requires skills, talents and experiences he or she does not have in sufficient supply and neither does the organization. This book is designed to help these leaders to see their organization in a new light – as a garden designed for a particular harvest, growing in changing environments and different seasons.

About This Book

How to Use this Book

This guide is designed to be a handbook, full of useful ideas and tools for handling all kinds of organizations, people and situations. It will also prepare the leader to train others in their organization. It will help everyone grow personally and professionally. However, it is only one of many tools and tactics available.

These include things such as the following:
- Phone calls - ongoing communication with others on the team, operating partners, etc.
- Websites
- Site visits

Structure of this Book

- *Prologue: The Nurturing Leader and Purpose of this Book* - The big picture; why capacity building is important for organizations around the world.

- *Introduction: Why Leaders Need Help* – Why is it vital that organizations be developed?

- *About this book* - Unique features and tools for planning, taking action and fueling growth.

- *Welcome to the Garden* – The organization as a garden.

- *Role of Consultants* – Getting outside help

- *Seasons of the Garden* – Stages of organizational development.

- *Appendix* – Gardening Guide's Toolkit: compendium of resources.

Elements & Tools

Sunshine: Insights and ideas. Nothing will grow without sunlight.

Spade: Useful tools for preparation and assessment. All ground needs to be prepared before it can be used.

Water: Processes to fuel growth. All plants need fuel to grow.

Rake: Problems to watch out for. Weeding is essential to make room for plant growth.

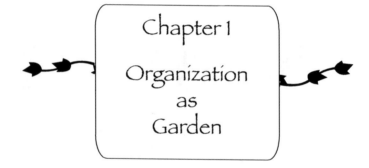

Chapter 1

Organization
as
Garden

Organization as Garden

Like a garden, organizations are teeming with many types of living things, systems, relationships and activity - all co-existing with each other. Like a garden full of life, a healthy organization bears fruit. It has all the ingredients needed to fuel growth - in all the right amounts at the proper time.

Organizations, like gardens, require continual attention, including careful planning, monitoring and weeding. Without this attention, they become a mess. Before you know it, the plants will stop bearing the fruit that was expected. Weeds will be growing everywhere and the soil will become depleted.

Systems

Organizations, like gardens, are complex and cannot be understood by simply examining and analyzing each part. They experience problems that involve helping many people see the "big picture" and not just their part. Systems can also be helpful at addressing recurring problems, whose solutions are not obvious, or those that have been made worse by past repair attempts. But organizations are more than systems. They are living, breathing entities that grow and change continually, and they require someone to look after them. That makes organizations very different than mechanical systems.

"Organizations are more than systems. They are living, breathing entities that grow and change continually."

Tending to the Garden

Like gardens, organizations cannot grow effectively on their own - they need people to lead and manage them. Someone has to determine what kind of garden is going to be grown. Is it going to be a vegetable garden or a flower garden? If it is vegetable, what kind should be produced? Is the soil and climate right for what is going to be grown? How will the workers determine if the plants are growing well? Like a garden, an organization needs someone in charge of it, and workers to tend it.

Due to history and circumstance, the gardener and workers may not have all the skills and resources to accomplish their goals. They may realize they could use outside help. They may also see the need for outside parties to provide resources like seeds and water to nourish them. Help comes from many sources. People with different skills, such as knowledge and experience about how to grow beans in acidic soil, may be needed. Or perhaps a special kind of fertilizer or other resources would enhance the garden's productivity. It may take someone, such as a consultant, to connect the gardener to these specialized forms of help.

Weedy Problems - Overall Signs of Trouble

Like gardens, organizations can become a mess:

• *Wrong outcomes* - The expected outcomes are not being achieved. Sometimes, no fruit is being produced.

• *People are wasting their time*, busy doing the wrong things. The wrong product or service is being delivered.

• *Lack of alignment* - People are going around the system. Informal networks have become the predominant way of getting things done, rather than following formal procedures and policy.

• *Inefficiency* - Products and services are not being delivered effectively or on time.

• *Disconnects* - People in the organization have an uncertain feeling. They know something is wrong but don't know what it is. They're not sure what they are supposed to do. Or there's disconnect between what they're doing and what the boss thinks they're doing.

• *Unhealthy culture* - Too often, there's finger-pointing. People are accusing each other of neglecting their duties or being ineffective.

• *Expectational drift* - The frontline worker questions the value of the management and vice-versa. They are out of touch, while management is frustrated because the frontline workers are not meeting the managers' expectations. (Joel Christie)

What weedy problems are occurring in your organization?

5

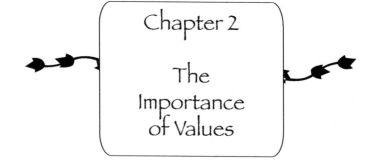

Chapter 2

The
Importance
of Values

The Importance of Values

Do values really matter or do leaders simply pay lip service to them? If they are important, how does an organization bring those values to life? Where do such values, which can be so mysterious and unpredictable, fit into the strategic plan and in the everyday life of the organization? Ideally, if a leader were to develop a new organization, he or she would go through the following stages:

Stage One: Identify Values. As important as it is for an organization to produce results, values must come first. The leader, with the input of his Board, senior management and stakeholders inside and outside the organization must be able to articulate, reinforce and practice these values. Then the organization must also stake them out officially.

This is why a vision and mission statement needs to reflect core values and how the organization will actually implement them. These statements can be the guiding light to people at all levels, and compared to actual practices to ensure they are being lived out.

For example, The Boeing Company summarized its values in the slogan "Forever New Frontiers". Cadence Design Systems Inc. also aimed high with their slogan question "How Big Can You Dream?" Another optimistic slogan example is L.M. Ericsson's: "Taking You Forward". If an organization's mission statement says that they take pride in the quality of their product, but tolerate shoddy work due to costs or time constraints, then their employees and customers are receiving inconsistent messages. If an organization says its employees are of prime importance, but they are abused, the values are being forsaken. If an organization states that it values innovation, but employees are discouraged from coming up with and trying new ideas and punished for taking risks, then it is not living out its values.

What is the purpose of your organization? List the values that underline this purpose. How are these values practiced in the everyday life of the organization? Are they practiced in every level and section of the organization?

Stage Two: Define Purpose. It may seem obvious, but organizations sometimes neglect their purpose - why they exist. Furthermore, they need to create goals and objectives that specify how the organization is going to accomplish its purpose. That means clarifying outcomes that reflect the values.

Stage Three: Clarify Decision-making. As a way of staying on track, an organization also benefits greatly from defining the decision-making processes that will live out its values. For example, if the organization values input from employees, but does not use the aggregate wisdom of employees and instead overrides that input, then it appears that the leaders are only giving lip service to these values.

There is a time to gain input and a time for action, but they need to cohere. A common problem, for example, is when employees are given responsibility without authority, having to check back with their supervisors before any decisions can be made or carried out. Here is another problematic example: an organization states that it will include quality people with the right skills and experiences, but when a key position opens up, the boss's favored child or friend, unsuitable for the position, is selected.

"There is a time to gain input and a time for action, but they need to cohere."

There must be consistency and alignment between the stated values and the everyday life of those in the organization. Misalignment creates uncertainty and confusion, and may lead to dissension.

Stage Four: Develop a Work Plan. Articulate how the organization will carry out decisions in alignment with its values. Employees may need to adapt their actions based on unpredictable events along the way. In these situations, employees must be able to make decisions and report them without being held back from adapting. Even if an organization values its employees and includes consensus building into its processes, it may fall back upon arbitrary decision-making by supervisors when problems come up - which are inevitable. If this becomes the rule, instead of the exception, then the organization appears hypocritical.

People are creative and some may even be crafty at times. Organizations and their structures, processes, and programs, therefore, tend to grow and change, like plants in a garden seeking nourishment and light as time goes on. That is all well and good when a garden is bearing fruit as expected, but what about when the harvest falls short or when other things get out of whack? And how do you determine the source of the problem?

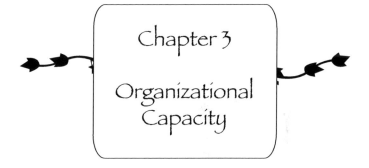

Eight Key Ingredients

There are eight key ingredients to effective organizations. They are the building blocks of capacity. By assessing them, leaders can determine which aspects of their organization need attending.

1. Leadership and governance - Lead gardener(s): The Board of an organization sets and maintains direction, develops policy and provides oversight, while monitoring, controlling and bringing accountability. Senior management is responsible for carrying out that direction and reporting to the board.

2. Strategic Plan and Business Model - Garden Plan: What kind of garden does the leadership want, what will it look like in the future, what will be produced, and how will it be produced? These essential components represent the vision, mission, values, overall strategy and defined outcomes and impact.

3. Programs and Services - Work Plan: What will it take to bring about this production? This involves project management - timeline, deliverables, who is responsible for what, accountability measures and budget. It also involves key stages of achievement with specific deadlines for each target milestone. This means times of celebration when different areas in the garden bear fruit.

4. Systems - Life in the Garden: The interaction of many parts creates a whole system, including processes and procedures. There are many situations requiring systems (e.g. HR or financial management). How does the organization manage the flow of water (their resources) making sure there is enough, and that it is going to the right plants until harvest? This relates to:

- The methods in which financial records are kept, income and expenses managed, cash flow analyzed and overseen, etc.
- Complex situations that involve helping many parties see the "big picture" and look beyond their part of it.
- Systems which can be very helpful at addressing recurring problems or those that have been made worse by past attempts to fix them.
- Issues where an action effects (or is affected by) the environment surrounding the issue, either the natural environment or the competitive environment.
- Problems whose solutions are not obvious.

5. Hardware and Software - Tools: Good maintenance is essential. (e.g. IT, telecommunications – like spades, rakes, hoses, and sometimes a backhoe).

6. HR - the Workers: This is a key but often overlooked component in an organization. Does the organization have the right workers with the right skills doing the right jobs? Are they organized effectively and are they tending to the plants? Are they communicating with each other effectively, especially if and when they need help? These imply relevant staff selection, orientation, staff development, retention, and performance appraisal.

7. Organizational Marketing - Product Sales: Another obvious but often-problematic area. Does the organization have an effective market for its products and services? Is the organization in touch with its clients and delivering the services they want? If they want sweet peas, it doesn't make sense to try and sell them onions. It is vital that an organization clearly identifies and maintains a healthy relationship with its clients, in touch with their needs and interests, communicating and promoting the right programs and services.

8. Fundraising - Nutrient Source: Without an effective method of finding an ongoing source of water and nutrients, a garden will soon die. In organizational terms: does it have trusted relationships with its suppliers of resources – its funders? That raises the questions about the management of those relationships. In other words, an organization needs a feasible fund development plan with financial goals, and strategic, effective fundraising strategies (e.g. engagement of major donor and stakeholders, ongoing reporting and relationship management).

Capacity Building – Defined

What does "capacity building" actually mean?

Capacity building enables organizations to grow, become stronger and incresase their effectiveness.

How? Capacity building calls upon all members of the organization to give of themselves to help each other and in so doing, to benefit themselves and their organization.

Capacity building involves a broad range of approaches, including fundraising, management consulting, leadership training, coaching of staff and the development of strategic alliances.

Organizations need people with the gifts, abilities, resources, experience, and go-for-it attitude to apply their personalities, talents, knowledge and skills as they jointly fulfill the mandate of the organization.

Capacity building is ultimately about building people up.

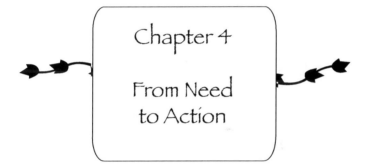

Chapter 4

From Need
to Action

From Need to Action

Before taking action, organizations must have a clear picture of the needs it is addressing. The best strategies work towards achieving the organization's end goals.

Assessing Organizational Capacity – HR Focus

To assess an organization's capacity to fulfill its mandate, it is very helpful for an organization to review each and every one of its eight aspects, and their level of capacity. Of prime importance is a review of the organization's Human Resources (HR) – its people and divisions, from top to bottom - and assess their capacity at each stratum. Here is an example of an HR assessment.

Human Resources	Clear need for increased capacity	Basic level of capacity in place
Staffing	Many key positions are unfilled, inadequately filled or there is high turnover	Most key positions are staffed although there are turnover or attendance issues
Board - composition and commitment	There are significant gaps in expertise, little diversity, commitment is low, meetings ineffective and attendance is infrequent	The Board provides some expertise but it is uneven, with only limited commitment, meetings of little effect and attendance somewhat irregular
Board - involvement and support	Little direction, support or accountability. Uninformed members; positions represented in title only.	Occasional direction, support and some accountability. Much effort needed to engage members.
CEO/ Executive Director and Senior Executive Team	Lacking vision and enthusiasm	Basic needs are met
Passion and vision	Low energy and commitment. Little vision or enthusiasm.	Engaged but not strategic. Responsive but not pro-active.

Adapted from McKinsey & Co.

Be on the lookout for issues related to confidentiality. Ensure all participants feel safe and secure. Also be sure to communicate that all findings will be aggregated, but no one will be named. That way, participants will be less concerned that they are "blowing the whistle" and might be blamed for it afterwards.

Table 1

To use this chart, mark an X in the cells where each division and level fits. Also ask your manager and staff where they see each division and level today. Compare perceptions and discuss the reasons behind them.

Moderate level of capacity in place	High level of capacity in place
Most key positions are filled and there is little turnover	All key positions are filled and there is little turnover and few attendance issues
There is some expertise and commitment. Meetings are usually effective and frequently attended.	The Board is highly qualified across a wide spectrum of areas, highly committed, and meetings are very effective and well attended.
Clear direction, support and accountability. Fully informed members. Responsive and engaged.	Strong direction. Champions to the cause. Enthusiastic and generously supporting the organization. Mutual respect and nourishing.
Some strengths, some weakenesses. Professional development needed.	Excellent role models, internally and externally.
Enthusiastic and visionary. Highly committed.	Enthusiasm is contagious. Visionary - and living out the vision. Compelling example to others.

Adapted from McKinsey & Co.

How Organizations Function

There are three sets of management "tools" at work in an organization that leaders can use to reduce uncertainty and create alignment. These must be continually adjusted.

Management "Tools"

- MISSION AND STRATEGY: These tools define what an organization is trying to accomplish and the key ways to fulfill its mandate.
- ORGANIZATIONAL STRUCTURE: These tools define how everyone is organized and how their efforts are clustered.
- HUMAN RESOURCES AND MANAGEMENT: These tools define who the organization involves — and how they are supported, developed, monitored and evaluated.

These managerial tools are available for use in each level of an organization. In other words, an organization can make things happen based on its mission, strategy, structure and people.

A garden is designed with a certain purpose in mind. Perhaps it is a small garden producing a wide variety of vegetables to feed a single family. That is its mission. Its strategy: to organize the family members around the cultivation and harvest of those vegetables. The environment that the family lives in will impact the implementation of that strategy. For example, if the family lives in the tropics, it will have different forces to deal with than if it lives near a desert.

Question: What is the environment that your organization inhabits? What forces are at work in that environment?

Systems, Systems, Systems

Systems are the building blocks of organizations. Noel Tichy, in his classic textbook about organizations, Managing Strategic Change, identified three kinds of systems. They include:

- TECHNICAL SYSTEMS: This type of building block focuses production and provision of service in the most effective and efficient manner.
- POLITICAL SYSTEM: This type of building block distributes the power within an organization, including how decisions are made and reported among all its levels and how resources are allocated based on those decisions.
- CULTURAL SYSTEM: This type of building block defines the reasons why the organization does everything the way that it does — which values are used to justify its approach.

All of these systems are driven by the mission and strategy of the organization.

In a garden operation, the tasks need to be clustered into jobs, such as planting seeds, watering and fertilizing. Skill is needed to carry out these tasks. But an organization also has to sort out how decisions are going to be made surrounding these tasks, such as who will be selected and how resources will be allocated.

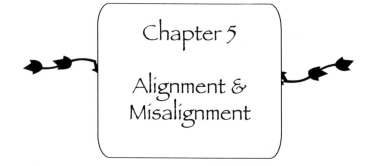

Chapter 5

Alignment &
Misalignment

Alignment and Misalignment

Misalignments can happen within these three sets of systems. If people are given a task but do not have adequate skills and knowledge to complete it, they may need skill enhancement. Incremental planning will increase efficiencies and effectiveness - helping the organization reach its existing goals and objectives.

Misalignment can also happen between these systems. In other words, there can be discrepancies between technical, political and cultural systems; misalignments between what, how and why an organization is doing what it does. That usually requires strategic change. For example, if staff are assigned a task (as part of the technical system) and are responsible for accomplishing it but are not also assigned the authority to do it (which is part of the political system) then the organization may have a serious problem.

This kind of misalignment may require a redistribution of power, reporting relationships, levels of authority and accountability mechanisms. Bringing about this kind of strategic alignment will redirect the entire organization, empowering staff to deliver the expected outcomes.

"Bringing about strategic alignment will redirect the entire organization."

Organizational Tiers

This set of tiers represent the levels within an organization. It includes three main tiers:

- STRATEGIC: This is the top level, including the Board of Directors, the President/Executive Director/CEO, and Senior Manager or Directors
- MIDDLE MANAGEMENT: In this level are the middle managers and supervisors responsible for ensuring that results are achieved in each area of effort.
- OPERATIONAL MANAGEMENT: These are team leaders on the frontlines or in operations to support the teams.

In a traditional organization, the head gardener or owner, and other people who have a vision for what the garden is to be, are found in the top level. Below them are the people who watch over the work that is being performed. On the ground, to carry out all of the tasks necessary to bear fruit, are the workers who till the soil, the seeds and the plants, and decide how to treat them daily. They are also there to harvest.

 Misalignment between tiers - between strategic, managerial and operational levels - may require strategic change. In other words, when different tiers of an organization are attempting to reach different goals and outcomes, then people in the organization are probably working at cross-purposes. If frontline staff see themselves as feeding the poor, but senior management expects frontline workers to be equipping the poor to be more independent and responsible, then the organization may need to re-examine its expected outcomes and the business it is really in. Realignment may require incremental or strategic change.

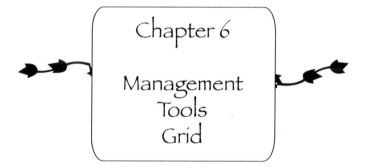

Chapter 6

Management
Tools
Grid

Management Tools Grid

Major components of an organization need to be in alignment for it to function effectively. The following grid can be used as a checklist, but also to see how the different dimensions are working together.

The kinds of questions being asked in the "Staff Questionnaire Template" approach alignment and misalignment within and between all three tiers. (e.g. "In general, what is your job? List the tasks that your perform. What information do you need to do these tasks? How do you get this information? From whom? Who influences what you do and the way you do your job? How have they influenced what you do?") For a fuller list of such questions, see the "Ask Staff" section on page 62.

Assessing Alignment

According to Tichy, there are many areas where alignment and misalignment can occur:

Managerial Areas	Mission/ Strategy	Organizational Structure	HR Management Process
Technical System	Assessing: Environment & Organization Defining: Mission & Fit of Resources	Differentiation Integration Aligning structure to strategy	Selecting and fitting people to roles Specifying performance criteria Measuring performance Developing staff
Political System	Determining who influences mission and strategy	Power: distribution & balance across groups of roles	Managing: succession & appraisal politics Designing & administering reward systems
Cultural System	Managing influence of values & philosophy on mission & strategy Developing a culture aligned with mission & strategy	Developing managerial styles aligned with structure Developing subcultures to support roles Integrating subcultures to form & organize culture	Selecting people to build or reinforce culture Team-building activities to mold organizational culture Managing rewards to shape culture

Adapted from Noel M. Tichy, 1983

Another powerful element in an organization is its people. Employees' attitudes, lifestyles, desires, issues, skills, knowledge and mindset can play into or create havoc in an organization.

How Systems Can Contribute to Misalignment

Conflict has to be discerned, addressed and managed. Otherwise, it can create uncertainty and confusion. If managed well, the forces creating conflict can be harnessed for good.

Technical Systems Pressures	Political Pressures	Cultural Pressures
Stagnation Declining productivity	Group politics Dependence (rather than interdependence) Demands for participation Equity issues	Demographics (e.g. male and female) Individualism vs. collectivism Demands of "profession" Expectational drift

Adapted from Noel M. Tichy, 1983

Conflict and misalignment in an organization does not spell doom. In fact, it can create positive results. All organizations have conflicts, and in the best scenario they are healthy for everyone involved.

As long as there is a clear, respectful and honest process used to resolve conflict, it can usually be managed for everyone's benefit.

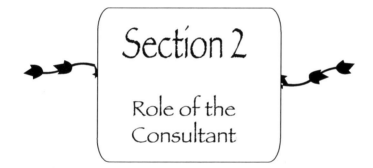

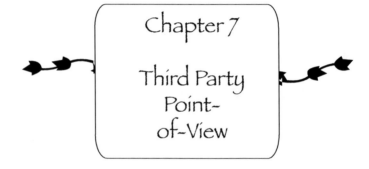

Chapter 7

Third Party
Point-
of-View

Western culture focuses on the importance of individual leadership, compelling leaders to work on their own. This is contrary to the thinking of many other cultures, including ancient cultures that treasure joint forms of leadership. Most cultures appreciate the value of diverse perspectives, looking to the group for vital differences of opinion.

Dialogue, disagreement and debate are essential parts of the process leading up to decision-making. For these reasons, it is essential for leaders who are going it alone, who lack a healthy form of debate among peers and elders, to look elsewhere for another, more experienced perspective. Tradition affirms the need to involve an unbiased, wise, third party when making key decisions.

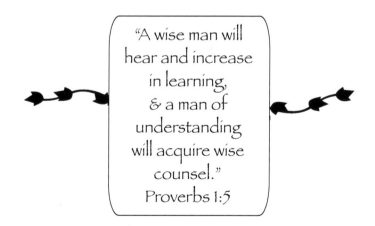

"A wise man will hear and increase in learning, & a man of understanding will acquire wise counsel."
Proverbs 1:5

Perspective - More than Sight

An experienced and trustworthy third party can provide more than a visual perspective. The consultant brings a new set of eyes, ears, mind and heart. In other words, there are many aspects to situations, which an outside party with no vested interest can provide. To be sure, leaders need to see and recognize the facts, but they also need to listen to the tone of what is being communicated by others. Of course, leaders also need to think about what they are assimilating. And they also need to tune into their own emotions and spirit - by themselves and with the help of others.

What is consulting? Often, it is about providing an objective view and passing along some clear thinking on whatever ails leaders and their organizations. It is about a fresh set of eyes - seeing what is really going on. It is not just about giving answers. More often it's about asking people the right questions. A good consultant really listens to what others have to say, helping them hear themselves and others.

Providing perspective is about discerning the situation, determining the real problem and sorting it out together. It means coming alongside people and helping them find their own answers. It goes beyond giving advice. A consultant equips others to handle situations for the long-term. Before long, the consultant does not have to provide advice, because the people they help become better equipped to find their own answers.

Nonetheless, information alone does not make the difference much of the time. Providing perspective is also about demonstrating the right way to interact and move forward. This brings inspiration, encouragement and provides support. As well, it's about developing character, modeling confidence and showing how to stick with it.

The task at hand for a consultant will vary depending on the person, role, task, purpose, etc. of each partner. Sometimes, the consultant is an engager, sometimes a mentor, sometimes a broker.

Question: what aspects of your organization could use an objective, third-party review? What are you having trouble discerning?

Experts vs. Advisers

Consultants are often seen as outside parties that are parachuted into situations to assess difficult situations and provide solutions. They are also viewed as experts who arrive with all of the answers, which they pass along and then leave. This form of consulting can be very helpful. For the long-term, however, an adviser is often what is needed. The adviser provides more than simply expertise. The adviser is also better suited to a wide variety of ongoing leadership needs.

Jagdish Cheth and Andrew Sobel in *Clients for Life*, summarize the difference between experts and advisers:

Experts	Advisors
Have depth	Have depth and breadth
Teach	Listen
Provide answers	Ask great questions
Develop professional trust	Develop professional and personal trust
Control	Collaborate
Supply expertise	Supply insight
Analyse	Analyse and synthesize

Consulting, when approached as an expert role, has many traps. The role brings many temptations, including arrogance. Anyone presented as an expert needs to be very careful to limit his or her activities to the narrow scope of that expertise. Otherwise, the consultant will end up delving into many areas far beyond that expertise. Rather, a consultant must be a link to answers. There are many sources of expertise that a consultant needs to draw upon, the least of which might be his or her own.

Key Roles

 Efforts to bring about successful change often include several key roles, including the initiator, the champion, the change agent, the sponsor and leaders. Organization-wide change in corporations should involve the Board of Directors. Whether the Board's members are closely involved in the change or not, they should at least be aware of the change project and monitor if the expected results are being achieved.

During various phases of change, the consultant may have different roles: agent of change, facilitator, broker, messenger, adviser, expert, mentor, friend, advocate and coach.

Since organizations are like gardens, there are different phases of capacity building. The consultant, if tuned to the needs of organizations, must help leaders address harvesting, planting new seeds, watering, fertilizing, spade work, weeding and so on. Some issues consultants need to consider:

- There are many seasons - beware of the easy fix

- Make good with what has been given to you and your client, not what you wish would be given to you

- Most organizations are more like a chaotic emergency response team than a well-oiled machine like IBM. Be realistic in your expectations and interventions.

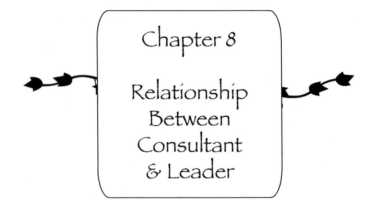

Chapter 8

Relationship
Between
Consultant
& Leader

Relationship between consultant and leader

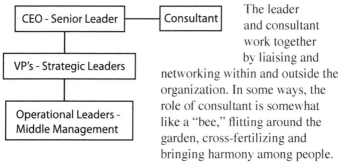

The leader and consultant work together by liaising and networking within and outside the organization. In some ways, the role of consultant is somewhat like a "bee," flitting around the garden, cross-fertilizing and bringing harmony among people.

The consultant is a builder of relationships. Doing that involves going between tiers, looking for alignments (and misalignments), going between projects, getting an idea of the whole and looking at ways to improve connections between parts.

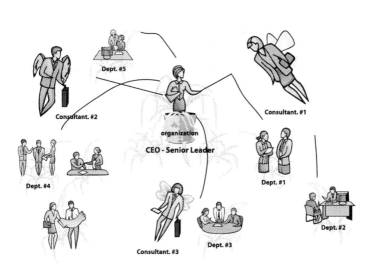

Adapted from Gareth Morgan

As this illustration points out, the consultant spends most of his or her time networking and transferring ideas, facilitating discussion, adding a certain amount of influence and encouraging everyone involved to move forward, all in a timely fashion.

The consultant must interact with a wide variety of people in an organization, including its operating partners and resource partners. He or she liaises between key contacts collecting information, probing for answers, bringing findings, recommendations, and connecting people and processes along the way.

 Agreeing to Work Together

It is vital that everyone in an organization, especially key leaders, have clearly defined roles, relationship and expectations. Other vital areas:

- Assessment of match of staff to their roles
- Openness to change
- Level of commitment
- Clarity of decision-making processes

See Appendix for more resources.

As important as it is that an organization defines its go-forward process, the consultant must also define his or her role and relationship with the client organization at the outset, and their mutual expectations. This is best set out in formal fashion — in a written agreement.

Professional Services Agreement (SAMPLE)

Agreement dated Aug. 20, 2009 between Consulting Company ("CC") and Your Organization ("YO.")

1. **CONTRACT:** YO agrees to contract CC to provide organizational development services, and CC agrees to perform, upon the terms and conditions herein specified, organizational development services for YO.

2. **TERM:** The Term of this agreement shall commence on Start Date and shall continue until End Date. This Agreement will be renewed for an additional 12-month period by Interim Date, unless otherwise stated by YO or CC, terms subject to negotiation.

3. **SERVICES:** Consulting Company, employing its staff, associates, facilities, technical capabilities, donors, and community contacts will commit to performing the following services for YO, between Start Date and End Date:

   - Organizational development of YO, which might include:
     - Consultation services: advise, assess, research, write and plan numerous areas of organizational development as needed, such as:
       - strategic plan and business model
       - governance structures
       - relationship with YO and sister organizations
       - human resources
       - financial management
       - project management
     - Joint consultation and ongoing communication with YO President (Your Name)
     - Liaison with associated professionals, such as lawyers, accountants, and other consultants to facilitate the organizational development process
     - Liaison with appropriate government bodies and political representatives to facilitate the incorporation process
     - Leadership development: selection, recruitment, hiring and orientation of YO leaders, such as:
       - President or CEO
       - Board of Directors
       - Others, as needed
   - Other duties as needed to fulfill these responsibilities

4. **TIME COMMITMENTS:** CC agrees to provide continuous service to YO as needed to fulfill this Agreement.

5. **FEES AND DISBURSEMENTS:** As full and complete consideration for CC's services and CC's undertakings hereunder and for all rights granted to YO hereunder, subject to CC's full compliance with the terms and conditions of this Agreement, YO agrees to pay CC as follows:

> **SERVICE FEES**: The sum of $X,XXX plus GST (X,XXX Dollars) per month.
>
> **OPERATIONAL COSTS**: YO agrees to provide use of an office, telephone, Internet, e-mail, printing, and other daily operational requirements, as well as use of a laptop computer, video production and post-production hardware and software.
>
> **EXPENSES:** YO to provide for pre-approved cost of computer hardware, office, domestic and international travel, long-distance phone, and public relations.

These Fees and Disbursements will be paid monthly net 30 days for the duration of the Agreement on the last business day of each month.

6. **CONFIDENTIALITY:** YO and CC agree that the terms of this Agreement are confidential.

7. **RESULTS AND PROCEEDS OF SERVICES:** YO shall be entitled to and shall solely and exclusively own, in addition to CC's services hereunder, all results and proceeds thereof (including by not limited to all rights, throughout the world) of any use of Plans, be it multimedia, Internet, broadcast, non-theatrical, print, promotional or otherwise.

8. **REPORTING RELATIONSHIP:** CC will report to Your Name, President, YO.

9. **PORTFOLIO:** CC shall have the right to use materials, documents and plans created for YO for CC's portfolio/professional purposes.

10. **EXPLOITATION:** YO shall always have the right to use and display any and all writing, designs and images created for YO for strategic marketing, development, fund development, advertising and publicity.

Signed and agreed to by the undersigned as of Date.

_____   _____
Your Name   Consultants Name
President/CEO - Your Organization   President - Consulting Company

Stages of Relationship

Consultant-client relationships often change
with time:

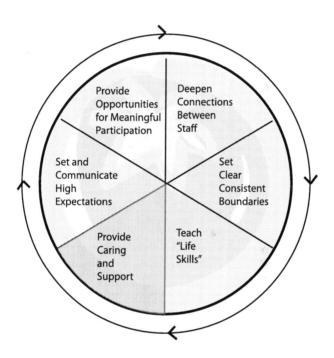

Provide Opportunities for Meaningful Participation

Deepen Connections Between Staff

Set and Communicate High Expectations

Set Clear Consistent Boundaries

Provide Caring and Support

Teach "Life Skills"

In order to play these essential roles in a trusted fashion, the
consultant needs the authority, ear and support of the leader, his
board and senior management.

A clear understanding of the terms of reference is also crucial.
To formalize that understanding, it also makes sense to define the
relationship, roles and expected results in an agreement as soon
as possible.

Job description(s)

According to McKinsey & Co., capacity building may involve many specific types of jobs, such as:

Organizational Assessment Consultant

This role may involve:

- Assessing the organization's capacity/capability to undertake and successfully deliver a project, an initiative or a change in the context of the overall program or portfolio program or portfolio priorities;

- Advising Senior Management on a range of issues affecting the organization's ability to achieve the project's business objectives;

- Identifying opportunities for organizational improvement;

- Assisting in the prioritization and assignment of organizational improvements;

- Developing and/or implementing an organizational improvement plan;

- Managing the implementation of an organizational improvement plan to identify, analyze, plan, track and control organizational improvements on a continuous basis for the project;

- Coaching, mentoring and training the organization to perform any of the above.

Group Facilitator

This role may involve:
- Group problem solving and decision making;
- Strategic planning;
- Team building;
- Participatory planning;
- Idea generation/Experiential learning;
- Large group facilitation;
- Training, mentoring and coaching;
- Leadership training;
- Electronic meeting support;
- Focus groups/Discussion moderation;
- Group process consultation;
- Information systems development.

Business Architect Consultant

This role may involve:
- Establishing the set of policies and rules governing the organization's actual and planned arrangements of computers, data, human resources, communication facilities, software and management responsibilities;
- Conducting an assessment of the project's business architecture, process and performances;
- Recommending changes to improve operational performance;
- Ensuring consistency and integration with the organization's architecture and business strategies;
- Evaluating the feasibility of the architecture and technologies related to a business change;
- Identifying risks associated with the architecture and technologies and recommending risk mitigation;
- Advising Senior Management on trends and emerging technologies and their impact on the organization's architecture and business strategies;

- Recommending alternative solutions, methodologies and strategies;
- Assisting in the prioritization and assignment of architectural improvements;
- Developing and/or implementing architectural improvement plans;
- Managing the development and implementation of an architectural improvement plan;
- Coaching, mentoring and training the organization to perform any of the above.

Organizational Design Consultant

This role may involve:
- Analyzing business functional requirements to identify information, procedures and decision flows;

- Reviewing existing work processes and organizational structure to determine their efficiency and effectiveness;

- Providing expert advice in developing and integrating new organizational models to eliminate information and process redundancies;

- Identifying and recommending new organizational structures;

- Identifying organization for re-design - prototyping potential solutions, providing tradeoff information and suggesting a recommended course of action;

- Providing expert advice on and/or assisting in implementing organizational changes;

- Planning, developing and organizing the policies and procedures of these establishments;

- Identifying the required modifications to the automated processes;

- Documenting workflow;

- Providing expert advice in defining new requirements and opportunities for applying efficient and effective solutions - identifying and providing preliminary costs of potential options.

"Above all, a great consultant is a humble servant committed to clients and their success, able to adapt and bring resources as needed, and to come alongside leaders as they take on difficult, ever-changing challenges and unpredictable opportunities."

Johari Window

 A popular psychology exercise from the 1960s helps to visualize how different perspectives interact. In this exercise, window #1 is the window out of which an individual sees his or her world. Some things in the view out an individual's window may not be obvious to him or her (even though they may be obvious to almost everyone else). Three of the four windows in this exercise cannot be seen from the individual's perspective. An individual is essentially blind, most of the time, to 75% of what is occurring. The good news is that these blind spots can be identified and clarified readily with the input and help of trusted advisors.

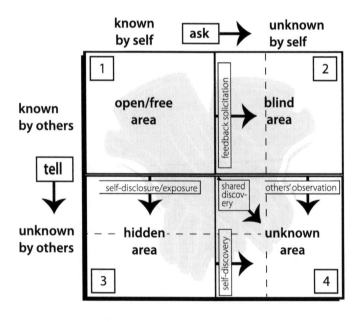

Adapted from Joseph Luft and Harry Ingham

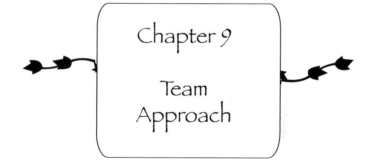

Chapter 9

Team
Approach

Team Approach

No one person can be all things to all people. Even the most talented and experienced leader needs others to play key roles in an organization. With time and with many resource people at their disposal who bring their own unique gifts, passions, skills and experience, leaders can build a team that will build a legacy within.

Discerning *Your* Gifts and Place on the Team

It's important for everyone to take the time to assess his or her gifts and talents - what you were made to do. A good exercise is to step back for a few minutes and do a personal assessment.

Gifts Assessment Exercise – Sample

Characteristics, gifts and hopes that you bring today - **SAMPLE**
Personal characteristics: Humor; enthusiasm, persistence; perfectionism; fresh ideas and passion; energy; prioritization; commitment dedication, patience, creativity. Goals: be able to adapt; show humility; have good health; bring sense of fulfillment; make a difference; share ideas.
Gifts: Understand clients and be aware of their needs; a strong background in design, planning, implementing; creativity; resiliency; steadfast determination; time; passion for clients served; commitment and reliability; being approachable; the belief that what I am doing is right and good; energy, motivation and attention to detail; following through.
Hopes: That others, including the next generation will become aware of the depth of needs among us. Hoping that our skills will be utilized and to share those skills with others. Hoping for happy, healthy, participating client population. Hoping for strong, resilient organizations and matching resources. Continuing to provide support for mind, body and spirit. Listening to changing needs of members. Hoping that we will learn from these seminars and go away with new ideas, friends and phone numbers.

Question: How would you describe your characteristics, gifts and hopes?

What I bring today
My Personal Characteristics:
My Gifts:
My Hopes:

Section 3

Seasons of
the Garden

"For everything there is a season, and a time for every purpose under heaven." Ecc 3:1

In the same way as a garden changes from season to season, an organization changes as well. It is helpful if leaders and managers are able to identify the different seasons of their organization:

 Winter*: This is a time when there is not much growth but plenty of light, reflection and visioning. It is a season of discernment for leaders and managers. This involves processes of evaluation and analysis - refining plans and birthing new ideas.

 Spring: This is a time of preparation: getting ready to make plans and ideas that emerged out of the winter season real.

 Summer: This stage brings growth. It involves nourishing: processes, resources and exercises to support and fuel growth. There is usually also some weeding that needs to be done, in which the consultant assists in overcoming and minimizing problems in the garden - internal and external - that need to be dealt with.

 Fall: This is a season that is often overlooked. The harvest is a time of celebration and thanksgiving, when key results and outcomes are acknowledged and saluted.

 Winter: The cycle continues with another season of light and reflection, enjoying the fruits of everyone's labor while thinking about how to improve for next year.

*Even in tropical climates where seasonal changes are not like the four described here, there are definite times of the year where activities are significantly less & both the people & the land enjoy some measure of rest.

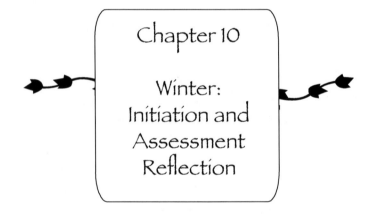

Chapter 10

Winter:
Initiation and
Assessment
Reflection

**Winter: Initiation and Assessment –
Reflection**

This is a time of scarcity, when activity is cut
back and staff takes time to reflect on what
the organization has done and what can be
improved upon. All too often, this is a season when a leader can
become depressed, defensive and even give up. If a leader can be
optimistic and enthusiastic while listening to staff and sorting out
what needs to be done next, this season can be a critical and life-
giving season of preparing for rebirth and regeneration; getting
ready for spring.

High Level Assessment of Your Organization's Needs

The garden metaphor is wrapped up with the notion that all of
the living components in the garden are intertwined to fulfill the
mandate of the organization. A high level assessment reviews
what is needed in all processes and all seasons.

In order to conduct this assessment, an organization needs to
review:

- **WHAT the people in the organization do**
  - Programs and services. Does the organization have
    the right people with the right talents using them in
    the right way to achieve the outcomes resulting from
    their efforts?

- **HOW the organization decides what to do**
  - Decision-making processes. For example, in the heat
    of an intense battle, an organization might need ONE
    person responsible for moment-by-moment decision-
    making. In this situation, decisions cannot include
    everyone's input.
  - Power to decide within all levels of the organization.

- **WHY the organization is doing what it does**
  - Values are used to justify an organization's actions. For example, when an organization involves its employees in a consensus-building fashion, it is based on the value that different people have different God-given gifts and talents, and have something to offer in the planning process.

Startup

Reflection is more than an intellectual process. In fact, it can be very emotional. The normal reflective process helps leaders and their key people move through important steps, that might flow from denial to depression or even hostility and on to gradual acceptance — gaining excitement about moving forward.

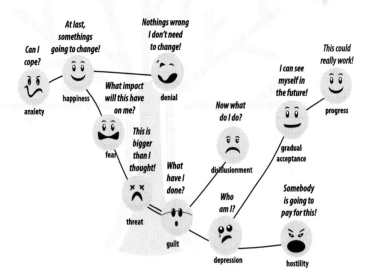

Adapted from Kubler Ross

The reflective process is a close look at the garden and its workers. It starts by having everyone consider working together, by mutual consent, and then having a good look at last year's harvest: was there real fruit or just plastic apples? It's also important to look at the ground: has the spadework been done for the spring, and if so, by whom?

Some things to look out for:
- Lack of commitment to change
- No clear outcomes
- Lack of comprehensive plan
- Lack of accountability measures
- Is the soil fertile? If not, why not?
- Water: is there a reliable source?
- Tools: Initial alignment of personalities, needs and gifts.
- How to build rapport: finding common interests.

Ultimately, the reflective process is about helping everyone find a good fit, and building trust.

Relationship Cycle
A trusting relationship is essential for the servant leader. In order for that to happen, rapport must be developed between the leader, his or her Board and then all of the staff.

The servant leader must be prepared to adapt his or her role and relationships with time as the process - and organization - progresses.

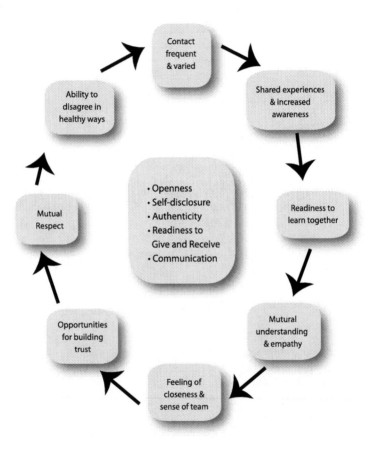

Adapted from Abraham Hicks

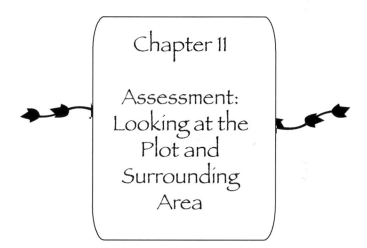

Chapter 11

Assessment:
Looking at the
Plot and
Surrounding
Area

Assessment: Looking at the Plot and Surrounding Area

This kind of review looks at all the critical factors to the success - and peril - of the organization generated from inside and outside the organization. It includes emergence of themes, personalities and dynamics as the map for the journey is formed.

It is vital to determine the level of support by the Board, senior leadership or middle management for an assessment prior to tackling it. A report with assessment, findings and recommendations assists the leadership to gain a common understanding of the big picture. The following tools will assist in the reflection and assessment process.

Environmental Scan

An environmental scan shows the big picture. The world at large is continually exerting forces on an organization, the people within it and the systems that the organization uses to stay on track. It is helpful to periodically scan these environmental forces.

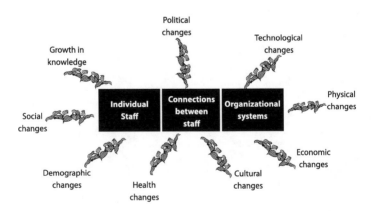

Strategic Questions for Strategic Leaders – including the Executive Director, Senior Management, Board and External Stakeholders

Probably the simplest and most effective way to assess the state or condition of an organization is to ask key questions of the leadership, inside and outside.

- *What is the change we wish to achieve in the world?*
- *What is our organization's role in realizing its vision?*
- *What social, economic, technological and environmental trends affect us?*
- *How do we attract the different resources required to advance and achieve our mission?*
- *What is the spirit of the organization?*
- *Is our staff enthusiastic? If not, why not?*
- *What strategic challenges or big questions are we currently facing?*
- *What actionable strategies must we form and implement to connect our mission to our stated goals and deliver real value or spiritual/social/physical impact to the community?*
- *How do we respond to demographic and social trends to ensure our programs and services are aligned with community priorities? (Economic, government, the church, social trends (e.g. poverty))*
- *How will we attract and retain skilled staff and volunteers and move to an integrated human resources strategy? What structural and operational changes will be required?*
- *How do we keep up with technological advancements in response to community priorities and consumer preferences?*
- *Are there other models of sustainability that we can explore? (Cost recovery for volunteer training, fee for service, social enterprise, innovations for facilities such as co-location, etc.)*
- *How do we ensure we can adapt to potential funding reductions and/or changes to investment priorities as a result of changes within the organization?*

- *How do we create an organizational identity that resonates with stakeholders and inspires others with whom we wish to establish a relationship?*
- *How do we establish and maintain our competitive advantage, increase our public profile and build brand awareness?*
- *How do we create a culture of philanthropy to advance our mission and create greater impact?*

Adapt and ask these questions of each division and level in your organization.

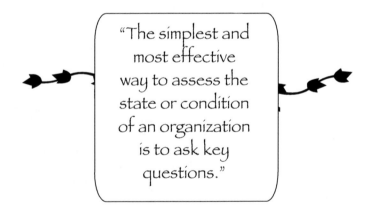

"The simplest and most effective way to assess the state or condition of an organization is to ask key questions."

Historical Highs and Lows

Go over the high and low points in the history of your organization with leadership/senior executives, middle management and frontline staff:

In order of occurrence in the history of your organization, note the positive experiences (above) and negative (below.)

Historical High and Low Points Scales

	+	
Beginning	————————————————	Present
	-	

For example, your organization may find that it has these highs and lows:

	Developed New Strategy		
			New Service Developed
	Initial Mandate & Funding		
Reorganization			
Beginning	Recruitment —————————————		**Present**
	Economic Downturn		Retirement of Founder

This simple but powerful tool allows participants to reveal what is important to them. Often, a striking trend is apparent. Different groups of people, be they strategic leaders, operational leaders, team leaders, Board members or stakeholders have very pointed thinking about the organization, which will be articulated in this process.

SWOT Analysis

The SWOT is a tool that has been used for many years. It is very effective for assessing what works and what doesn't, as well as identifying all kinds of opportunities and challenges.

STRENGTHS	
Examples of Strength criteria:	What do you and your department do well?
Capabilities	Where do you shine?
Leadership/Board	What sets you apart – your "distinctives"?
Position in the community	
Service model	What do others see as your strengths?
Strategic partnership	What role do you play that no one else does?
Competetive advantage	
Financial position	
Processes	
Marketing	
Fundraising	

OPPORTUNITIES	
Examples of Opportunities criteria:	What good opportunities are open to you and your department?
Room for growth	Who could be right to team up with?
New markets	
Strategic partnerships	What trends could you take advantage of?
New IT developments	
New and improved ideas and strategies	How could you turn your strengths into opportunities?
Learning and skill developments	What plans do you have to make that a reality?

Be on the lookout for the following potential pitfalls:
- Weak Board
- Lack of or indecisive leadership
- Lack of trust between leadership and frontlines
- Weak financial management

WEAKNESSES	
Where could you and your department improve?	Examples of Weaknesses criteria:
	Disadvantages of proposition
Where do you have fewer resources than others who do similar work?	Gaps in capabilities
What are others things people likely see as weaknesses?	Weakness in reputation, presence or reach
	Known vulnerabilities
	Shortage of cash
	Shortage of staff
	Lack of continuity
	Lack of competencies
	Low morale
	Undefined processes or lack of systems
THREATS	
What trends could harm you and your department?	Examples of Threats criteria:
	Political forces
What is your competition doing that could adversely affect your organization?	Government changes
	Environmental effects
What threats do your internal weaknesses expose you to?	IT developments
	Loss of key staff
What are you unprepared to handle?	Lack of sustainable funding
	Economic changes - downturn

Discernment

Ask yourself, your Board and staff these questions and compare answers.

1. *What is the spirit of the organization — between people, team-members and units?*
2. *How do people relate to each other?*
3. *What kind of body language is used in meetings between leadership and frontlines? How do the leaders treat each other?*
4. *How do the frontline employees treat each other?*
5. *How do stakeholders outside of the organization feel about it?*
6. *How do you feel about these matters?*

Ask Staff

Some of this can be very simple: just ask people how it's going! When done on a regular basis, this can help you discover organizational alignments and misalignments. Use it to compare the expectations and issues of staff at each echelon of the organization, including leaders (and senior management), middle management and operations (including frontline staff.) Watch for expectational "rifting and drifting."

Questions you can use to check the pulse and momentum of your staff:

1. *In general, what is your job? List the tasks that you perform.*
2. *What information do you need to do these tasks? How do you get this information? From whom?*
3. *Who influences what you do, and the way you do your job? How have they influenced what you do?*
4. *Who evaluates you? What criteria are used to evaluate how you have been doing your job? How is your performance evaluated? Does anyone else influence the evaluation of your performance?*

5. *Do you have a clear understanding of the structure of this organization? Do you think these reporting relationships are appropriate? How could they be improved?*

6. *How does one get ahead in this organization? Do you think this is appropriate? Why?*

7. *Do you know if there is a Mission Statement for this organization? What is it? Would it help to have one? Why? Who do you think should develop the Mission Statement? How should it be developed? Who should have a say in what the Mission Statement should be?*

8. *What in your opinion are the major goals of this organization? What are the major values that seem to be important in this organization? What are the values underlying the way your team or department operates? Are these values consistent, and are they consistent with your own values? If they are inconsistent, how can they be realigned?*

9. *Is there an informal network in this organization? How does it affect you?*

10. *What do you expect from your job? What do you expect from the management? What do you expect from this organization?*

11. *What do you think are the three most important things this organization has had to face over the last five years? How did it deal with each of them? What are the three most important issues this organization needs to face over the next three years?*

12. *How do each of these issues affect your work? Ideally, how would you like to see these issues resolved? Who needs to be involved? What do you fear might happen if these issues are not resolved?*

13. *In general, what changes do you think should be made to improve the organization now? Why?*

Once you collect the information, identify the major themes for each level and division of the organization. Report it and bring resolution with leadership and staff.

Adapted from Joel Christie

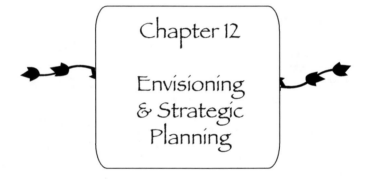

Chapter 12

Envisioning
& Strategic
Planning

Envisioning and Strategic Planning

Sometimes, this is the most exciting part of the effort - designing the future garden of products and services. But it can take a lot of spadework. Work backwards from the end goal of the organization: its vision and slogan.

Strategic Planning Process (Sample)

This process can be as simple or complex as everyone wants to make it. To expedite the process, it is best to define and limit the scope of the activities from the start, before it may get out of hand. (Also see Appendix for resources.)

This process often bears rich fruit: a Strategic Plan is a milestone for most organizations, if they do not already have one. It provides guidance to everyone for many years, and it can also bring great confidence and excitement.

Here is a sample strategic planning process for a large organization:

Tasks	Deliverables	Timeframe	Consultant time hrs
Meet with Board and executive staff to review process.	Presentation of an overview of the process. Review and clarification of the staff questionnaire.	Presentation Date - Day 1	3 hrs.
Meet with Executive Committee (Pres/CEO and senior management) to review progress and prepare for Strategic Planning Session and Environmental Scan	Ongoing updates on progress, incorporation of any special concerns and additional data into the planning process.	Days 2-15	3-9 hrs.
Research, analyze and write up findings.	Discussions of trends, issues with stakeholders, including political environment, sectoral analysis, collaborators, clients	Days 3-15	50 - 100 hrs.

Tasks	Deliverables	Timeframe	Consultant time hrs
Receive, analyze and summarize data from questionnaires.	In liaison with staff, conduct interviews and questionnaires, summarize the issues, factors and future expectations that the organization needs to address strategically. Build them into the Strategic Planning Session.	Days 3-15	50 - 100 hrs
Design Strategic Planning Session, review with Executive Committee, incorporate changes.	Outline of Strategic Planning Session with accompanying material	Days 16-21	5-10 hrs.
Facilitate Strategic Planning Session	Discussion of & consensus on: - Visions — positive vs. negative scenarios - Mission, goals, objectives - Organizational processes and structure	Days 22-23	16 hrs.
Prepare summary of findings & recommendations from Strategic Planning Session	Draft Strategic Planning document for review	Days 24-32	20 - 40 hrs.
Present draft report to Executive Committee & Board for review & comment	Meetings with Executive Committee & Board, discussion of final information to be incorporated	Days 33-37	6 hrs.
Collate, analyze & incorporate input from Executive Committee & Board into the final Strategic Planning document	Final document ready for distribution & implementation	Days 38-42	5 - 10 hrs.
	TOTAL	136- 170 days	102- 182 hrs.

The Envisioning Process

Dark Star/Bright Star Exercise

Everyone must have free will to envision and grapple with the future. They can envision a dark future or a bright future and it is important to identify the processes that would underlie both. To be realistic, we need to recognize and deal with dark future scenarios, and to encourage and build toward a bright future. These findings can be incorporated into the implementation plan, which will show how to identify things you must do to make the bright star a reality and to prevent the dark star from occurring.

Dark Star - The fears we bring with us today

Sample Fears
Continued staff turnover; low wages and benefits; shortage of core funding
Dysfunctional Board
Burnout of staff and volunteers
Difficulty bringing in boomers
Lack of board members
Not going to be in existence in 7-10 years
Concerns about maintaining /upkeep of facilities
Ways that clients/members will suffer if problems not addressed
Inability to act on best practices/goals when there is so much turnover
More isolated clients being less active in community - problem of transportation to the centre

My Fears

Dark Star - Future Scenarios: *What would a typical day look like if your worst fears came true?*

- Headline in the local daily newspaper
- Telephone messages - Whom are you calling? What are you saying?
- Emails - Who from? What about? What are your replies?
- Staff Meeting - Who is there? How are you greeted? Agenda for meeting? How does the meeting go?
- Annual General Meeting - Where? What happens? How do you respond?

What	Why – underlying reasons why these things occurred
	Top 5 Reasons why this overall negative scenario occurred - these reasons will be incorporated into your implementation plan to address risks

Bright Star – What will the future world look like if all your hopes came true?

Sample Gifts and Hopes that you bring today – sample
Gifts: Humor; enthusiasm, persistence; perfectionism; fresh ideas and passion; being able to prioritize; commitment, dedication, experience, patience, creativity.   **Hopes:** Be able to adapt; show humility; good health; bring sense of fulfillment; make a difference; share ideas
Gifts: Open-mindedness; work as a team; think outside the box   **Hopes:** Adequate funding; additional staffing; retention of existing staff; more volunteer participation; attract boomers; more advertising and media exposure; more core funding; adequate support; more active membership by those not currently active

Bright Star - Future scenario: *What would a typical day look like if your wildest dreams came true?*

- Headline in the local newspaper
- Telephone messages - Whom are you calling? What are you saying?
- Emails - Who from? What about? What are your replies?
- Staff Meeting - Who? Agenda for meeting? How does the meeting go?
- Annual General Meeting - Where? What happens? How do you respond?

What	Why – underlying reasons why these things occurred
	Top 5 Reasons why this overall positive scenario occurred - these reasons will be incorporated into your implementation plan to encourage a positive future

Question: Think of strategies for your organization that will result in your Bright Star coming true and preventing a Dark Star from transpiring. This will include strategies that will reinforce the best-case scenario as well as addressing the fears that you have identified.

_____

_____

_____

_____

_____

_____

_____

_____

Slogan

In the same way that Boeing summarized its values in the slogan "Forever New Frontiers", ask leaders to "boil down" their vision into a defining phrase that captures the essence of your Bright-Star Vision. This can help define aspects of the hoped-for future. It can also guide in the development of the Work Plan.

Mind Map

Draw a diagram with the Vision in the centre using the Slogan as shorthand for the Vision. Then develop three to five Bright Star Goals that, if fulfilled, will realize that Vision. Develop Objectives for each Goal, and sample Tasks to realize those Objectives. From these Tasks, a Work Plan is easily created which will spell out the critical tasks for the organization. Finally, develop a timeline and accountability measures for each task. The Dark Star scenario can be used to inform the accountability measures.

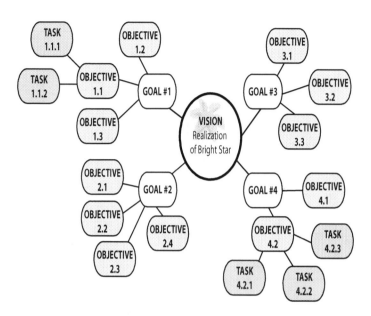

The leadership will now have a plan and consensus, which can be used to guide preparations for the next season - Spring.

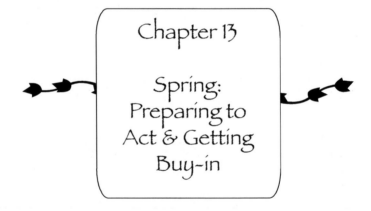

Chapter 13

Spring:
Preparing to
Act & Getting
Buy-in

Spring – Planning to Put the Vision and Mission into Action

Spring is a time of preparing everyone to carry out the Strategic Plan. It is a season of readying the soil and planting seeds and ideas, which will later bear fruit. This helps everyone get ready to make the key ideas from winter accepted and real.

For sustainable change to occur, all key stakeholders need to agree to the overall recommendations and decisions regarding implementation.

Sustaining Change Equation

The organization should now be ready to carry out the ideas and strategies developed in the previous season, with "buy-in" by everyone. Otherwise, the organization will be like rocky or shallow soil, unable to fully carry out the changes and growth.

Big Picture

The Strategic Plan encompasses the Vision and Mission. It is the Big Picture, and it informs the change process.

- This includes direction, strategies and framework. It answers key questions, such as "why change?" It is detailed, providing the Project Plan.
- It is important for people to understand how any proposed change fits within the large organizational Vision and Mission. The Big Picture inspires and aligns activity.
- If lacking, only short-term results will be achieved. Organizations can easily lose the strategic dimension needed for change if they ignore this process.

Question: Why should your organization change? What is driving this change? Which sections need change? Which sections do not need change?

....

_____

....

_____

....

_____

....

_____

Buy-In: Commitment, incentives, recognition and empowerment.
- Lasting change must take place in the hearts and guts of real people.
- A key to encouraging buy-in is to communicate, communicate, communicate (including listening!)
- If lacking, complacency, politics, delays, and turf protection tend to occur.

Question: Does everyone in your organization know that change is needed or is underway? If not, how do you think employees can be engaged to look at that change, deal with their fears related to it, and embrace the new direction?

....

_____

....

_____

....

Skills and tools: Human capital, development, equipment, space and work design.

- Nothing is as frustrating as wanting to change but lacking the skills or tools to do the job.
- If lacking, frustration, anxiety, dissatisfaction and safety issues can result.

Question: Where do you have adequate knowledge and skills? What knowledge and skills does your organization need to acquire?

_____

_____

_____

_____

_____

Manage Risks: Resistance, roadblocks, uncertainty and apprehension.

- When presented with change, it is natural for people to think of the downside and potential risks associated with change, many of which would have been identified during the Dark Star exercise. Openness and truth-telling are effective in articulating and managing these concerns.
- If lacking, pessimism, resistance and cynicism will start to show up.

Question: What fears are creating roadblocks and how can you address them?

_____

_____

_____

_____

_____

Action: Leadership, tactics, action plans, small wins and next steps.
- Success breeds success and builds confidence.
- It is imperative that leaders lead the organization through the change process.
- If lacking, blue-sky syndrome is often the result, including lots of talk but no action, rumours, lost morale and dissension.

Question: Do you have an action plan? Does your organization have the knowledge and skills needed to create the plan? If not, how are you planning to develop it? What kind of accountability is needed to ensure that these actions are taken?

_____

_____

_____

_____

_____

Lasting change: Improvement, implementation, transition, performance and behavior change.
- Quality and return on investment plus productive workforce will ultimately be the outcome.

Question: What kinds of methods do you need to use to bring this about? For example, how will you build lasting change into performance appraisals, events, meetings and reports?

_____

_____

_____

_____

_____

_____

Staging the Process

 To be successful, the Strategic Plan requires its own process, to enhance buy-in from all stakeholders. It is pieced together one stage at a time, based on the findings from the wide forms of assessment explained above. Above all, it's about making strategic choices that will affect the future of the organization. It helps greatly if, right from the beginning, it is settled which stakeholders should be consulted.

The strategic planning process in its entirety can seem quite onerous, often because it can be very complex and tedious if the boundaries are not very strict. Don't make it any more complex than it needs to be.

Putting the vision into action involves planting the seeds with the end in mind.

Strategic Planning Implementation Process – Key Stages and Considerations

Stages	Considerations
Define the organization's future direction: Develop a clear statement of future goals, which have consensus of leaders, staff and stakeholders.	The organization's purpose should mesh with the strategic goals of all departments and units. Keep the statement brief and easy to remember and understand.
Determine the competitive advantage and what is unique about the organization. Develop a concise description of why clients will use your products or services, and not others.	The advantages of your organization should have lasting value.
Set boundaries of pursuit and areas to focus on.	Although the scope of the process should be as focused as possible, make sure to include all key people and groups.
Define what the clients/customers want and need.	Sometimes, the details can make a big difference. Call on the help of product & service experts if needed.
Agree on a budget.	Be sure to get the input of the people who need the budget. The experts in finance may be able to clarify accounting matters and speed things up.

Our Stages	Key Considerations

It's never too late to do a reality check. Reviewing the plan periodically is wise, to see if the assumptions are still correct. Often, the plan may need updating - and reworking.

Having hashed out the need for change and a vision for the future, it's very important to decide what kinds of seeds to plant and how they are going to come into fruition. In other words, it's time to develop a Program Logic Model and Goal Attainment Scale for each project. These will clearly outline expected outcomes and accountability measures. It will also equip everyone involved to implement the plan. All relevant parties need to come to agreement on it, and it must be communicated to everyone impacted. It also makes sense to have those in authority agree on roles, milestones and accountability mechanisms.

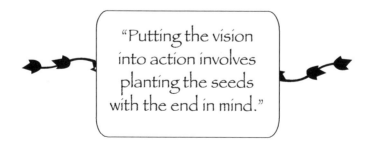

"Putting the vision into action involves planting the seeds with the end in mind."

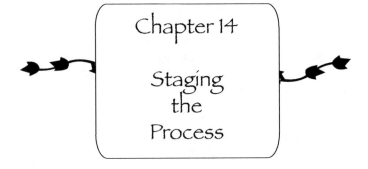

Chapter 14

Staging
the
Process

Situation Analysis - Sample

Situation	Organization: XYZ Literacy	Time-frame
XYZ is a country with 30 different languages. The national literacy organization has completed literacy programs for 10 languages and now needs to develop literacy in another 10 language groups using the experience and processes developed in the first stage. Technology has developed to expedite literacy work. Expectations have risen with the advent of new technologies. Performing literacy with manual systems, as before, would be cumbersome and slower. Now, computer skill development also has to occur. Computer systems, software and networks are needed to support this next stage.	PROJECT NAME: "Moving into the 21st Century: A Literate People": Developing Literacy Using Modern Tools to Meet Enhanced Expectations"	Pilot: 2010-2012

Describe your situation

Situation	Your Organization	Time-frame

Program Logic Model (SAMPLE)

MEASURES TO BE TAKEN	Inputs	Staff, Volunteers, Training, Oversight, Evaluation
	Activities	**Connect with local Schools, NGO's and Community Groups.** Build rapport with informal leadership of community, set up a Steering Committee comprised of representatives of the community, sub-groups, and participating community agencies.
		Assess Situation. In collaboration with the community leaders and others in the Steering Committee, gather information about the living situations of the ABC Language Group and from this, identify priority actions.
	Outputs	# of community group contacts # of meetings # of schools, NGO's and community organizations participating in this collaboration Baseline Report # of individuals and families participating in this assessment
ANTICIPATED RESULTS	Short-term Outcomes	Growing mutual trust, common agreement to collaborate, common sense of purpose between "Moving into the 21st Century: A Literate People":" to other schools, NGO's and community organizations and leaders of the ABC community.
		Baseline understanding of the demographics, education, skills and language profiles of the ABC Language Group and those currently working with them. Agreement on the most pressing issues and priorities for action.
	Intermediate Outcomes	Schools, NGO's and community organizations currently working with the ABC Language Group have their members enrolled in literacy classes and using materials developed.
		Those participating in the literacy classes affirm that the materials make sense in terms of their culture & daily lives.
	Long-term Outcomes	**ABC people read and write in the context of their own culture and daily life.**

Your Program Logic Model – Fill In

MEASURES TO BE TAKEN	Inputs	
	Activities	
	Outputs	
ANTICIPATED RESULTS	Short-term Outcomes	
	Intermediate Outcomes	
	Long-term Outcomes	

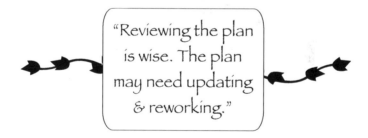

"Reviewing the plan is wise. The plan may need updating & reworking."

Implementation Readiness – The Action Work Plan

Using the findings from the Dark Star/Bright Star analysis, the leader, with help from a consultant, can identify barriers and risks which will be dealt with in the Implementation phase

 This tool articulates who does what by when. A budget should also be assigned. As well, it is useful to measure output along the way.

Table 1

			1a	1b	1c	2a
Project Leader: **Mr. Smith**	Periods Marked by:	Item #	1a	1b	1c	2a
		Priority	1	1	1	1
Tazmania		Task List	Board Development	Leadership Development	Financial Mgmt Syst. Dev't	HR Policy Development
	Day	Person Responsible				
Project ID #:		Begin Date	July 2008	Sept 2008	Oct. 2008	Jan. 2009
	Week	Target End Date	June 2009		Jan. 2009	
Organization		Final End Date				
XYZ	Month	Forcast Cost				
		Final Cost				
Project Name:		Initial				

Table 2

Project Leader: **Mr. Smith**	Periods Marked by:	Item #				
		Priority				
Country		Task List				
	Day	Person Responsible				
Project ID #:		Begin Date				
	Week	Target End Date				
Organization		Final End Date				
XYZ	Month	Forcast Cost				
		Final Cost				
Project Name:		Initial				

Reality Check #1: Session Rating Scale
The facilitator or consultant for the strategic planning process must regularly check to ensure that he/she is listening to the client and focusing in on what the client feels is important.

SESSION RATING SCALE

Name: _____

Position: _____

Date: _____

Please rate today's session by placing an "X" on the line nearest the best description of your experience

| I did not feel heard, understood or respected | Relationship | I felt heard, understood and respected |

| We did not talk about what I wanted to talk about | Topics | We talked about what I wanted to talk about |

| The leader's approach did not seem appropriate to me | Approach | The leader's approach seemed appropriate to me |

| Overall, there was something missing in the session today | Overall | Overall, todays session was right for me |

Adapted from the Institute for the Study of Therapeutic Change

Now that the organization has a strategic plan clarifying the vision and a logic model with expected outcomes, it needs to have a feasible implementation plan with milestones and assignments of responsibilities coming out of the strategic plan.

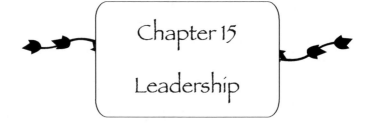

Chapter 15

Leadership

For a strategic plan to become a reality, leadership at all levels must make sure they are up to the task.

Leadership

It goes without saying, but in most cases, the most vital people in organizations are its leaders.

Leadership Attributes Analysis Tool

Each leader needs to take a good look at his or her strengths and areas of potential. A personal review process can be difficult for anyone, especially when peers are looking over one's shoulder. But it's worth it. Asking tough questions of oneself can be strength-based, affirming and encouraging, while opening doors to growth. It can also generate great insights that will benefit the individual, his/her co-workers, family, and the whole organization for years to come.

- What am I good at doing?
- What areas need to be enhanced?
- What skills are vital to performing my current job? How good am I at each skill area?
- What are the most critical skills for this type of leadership?
- If I am to advance, what skills do I need to develop further?
- What types of skills do I want to develop that are not listed that I would like to enhance?

It is best to remind each person to take note of their responses, to prepare them to take action later.

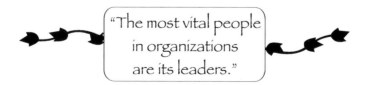

"The most vital people
in organizations
are its leaders."

The senior executive, his/her VPs and the Board of Directors, as has been said, are key. These are the "Strategic Leaders." But they are not the only leaders who count. Often, the middle management ("Operational Leaders") are also vitally important. The same goes for those people who lead others on the frontlines ("Team Leaders").

Like every other area of preparation and assessment, it often helps to review the leadership. Above all, engage them in assessing themselves at their skills & attributes, looking at what they need to develop or surround themselves with.

Strategic Leadership Attributes Test

What are the attributes of a Strategic Leader? Not only do they need to be competent in bringing about results, they also must be attentive to people, and effective in developing strategies for success. Strategic Leaders can assess themselves or be assessed by others using the test below. Score 1/5: very little competency; 5/5: extremely competent.

Gifts, Skills and Abilities	Competency Level				
Champion: brings about the right environment and top results	1	2	3	4	5
Influencer: affects a wide variety of others in a positive fashion	1	2	3	4	5
Decision-maker: carries out decisions in a wise and timely way	1	2	3	4	5
People-builder: equips, encourages and inspires others to their potential	1	2	3	4	5
Frontrunner: leads change in a pro-active fashion	1	2	3	4	5
Completer: brings about results in line with end goals	1	2	3	4	5
Tactician: not only develops strategic plans, but enables them to happen	1	2	3	4	5
Manager: organized, monitors results, and stays on track	1	2	3	4	5
Forecaster: provides foresight as part of the priority-setting, and reaches objectives	1	2	3	4	5
Team player: keeps people together, engages and comes alongside others	1	2	3	4	5

Adapted from Fiona Elsa Dent (2003)

Operational Leadership Attributes Test

The Strategic Leader keeps an eye on the big picture, stays in touch with external stakeholders and ensures that the overall goals are met. Conversely, the Operational Leader is much more involved in day-to-day supervision of projects, ensuring that areas of work are fulfilled and staff and client needs are met.

Here is the test for the Operational Leader:

Gifts, Skills and Abilities	Competency Level				
Champion: brings about the right environment and top results	1	2	3	4	5
Influencer: affects others in a positive fashion	1	2	3	4	5
Coach: lifts people up while achieving ends	1	2	3	4	5
People-builder: equips, encourages and inspires others to their potential	1	2	3	4	5
Self-Master: self-disciplined, aware of own skills and gaps, personally effective	1	2	3	4	5
Social Skiller: good with people, effective communicator	1	2	3	4	5
Broker: negotiator, change agent, adaptable	1	2	3	4	5
Decision-maker: carries out decisions in a wise and timely way	1	2	3	4	5
Operator: knows the organization's way of doing business, gets things done from inside and outside the organization	1	2	3	4	5
Team player: keeps people together, engages and comes alongside others	1	2	3	4	5

Adapted from Fiona Elsa Dent (2003)

Team Leadership Attributes Test

The Team Leader is on the "bleeding-edge" of frontline work. He or she has to make sure that the people handling daily tasks are on track, on time and on budget. Here, there is much more emphasis on the team and the job at hand. The Team Leader and the frontline people who face clients all day long are directly involved in seeing that the clients are serviced properly.

Here is the test for the Team Leader:

Gifts, Skills and Abilities	Competency Level
Champion: brings about the right environment and top results	1 2 3 4 5
Team player: keeps people together, engages and comes alongside others	1 2 3 4 5
Coach: lifts people up while achieving ends	1 2 3 4 5
People-builder: equips, encourages and inspires others to their potential	1 2 3 4 5
Self-Master: self-disciplined, aware of own skills and gaps, personally effective	1 2 3 4 5
Social Skiller: good with people, effective communicator, lots of "chemistry"	1 2 3 4 5
Broker: negotiator, change agent, adaptable	1 2 3 4 5
Operator: knows the organization's way of doing business, gets things done from inside and outside the organization	1 2 3 4 5

Adapted from Fiona Elsa Dent (2003)

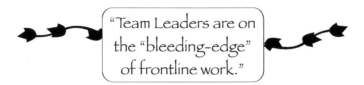

"Team Leaders are on the "bleeding-edge" of frontline work."

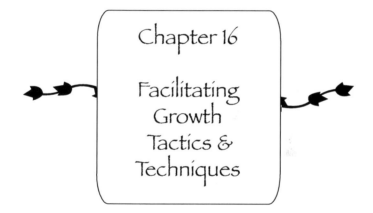

Chapter 16

Facilitating
Growth
Tactics &
Techniques

Facilitating Growth – Tactics and Techniques

There are a number of strategies and techniques to involve people in a "group-think" process, to develop their ideas, organize everyone's thinking, encourage decision-making and achieve consensus. These strategies can be used in all seasons. Though best done face-to-face in workshops with small groups, they can also be performed by teleconference, online or one-on-one.

How to Brainstorm

When done well, brainstorming involves all concerned in a fun and productive fashion. This is the basic recipe for an enjoyable and effective experience:

- Using a whiteboard, flipchart or Power Point Presentation, ask everyone in attendance to suggest a solution to the problem or challenge.
- Record all suggestions. Be creative in the way that ideas are described - use drawings, symbols, music and/or colour. Make the process fun and ensure ideas stand out.
- Organize ideas in conjunction with the strategic areas being focused upon.
- Challenge everyone to open up the treasure-chest of original thinking. Allow "crazy" ideas, both for fun and to warm people up.
- Continue until ideas become derivative. Then have participants score them so that the best ideas are selected and synthesized.
- Share the ideas in a lively fashion - involve everyone in celebrating the great insights and solutions that they have developed.

Everybody has a Great Idea

Participation is key to affirming everyone's unique gifts and personality. This exercise allows different ideas to be brought together in a graphic fashion, and often produces a "light bulb" experience. Try this fun exercise:

- Have everyone pair up or form groups of threes. Give each group some blank cards. Ask each group to record an answer to each of the key questions being asked. One short answer should be recorded on each card.
- Have each group pin their cards up on the wall underneath each question. After the facilitator reads them all aloud, have all participants together make decisions about how to arrange cards in clusters representing similar ideas. Eliminate duplicate ideas.

Distillation Exercise: Categorizing and Choosing (Decision-making) Exercise

Now, participants must together make sense of these collective ideas. Involve everyone in distilling, sorting and naming categories for each cluster. Brainstorm and settle on a definitive title – a phrase of one, two or three words - summing up the main idea in each category.

- In clear lettering, write the category titles on a card or sticky note above each cluster.
- Neatly re-organize the key ideas related to that category under each title.
- Allocate three colored dots to each participant. Have them vote for the ideas they like best using these dots. They may distribute their three dots any way they wish, putting one, two or three dots beside an idea.
- Count up the dots in each category. Tally and write the score in each category. Rank the top four or five.

Ask the group for feedback. See if they can agree to the prioritization of ideas.

De Bono Gets it Right Again: "Six Thinking Hats"

In his book *Six Thinking Hats* Edward de Bono came up with many brilliant yet fun ways of finding out what people are thinking. This is one of his best tools for involving people who think differently and who recognize different approaches to the same problem or challenge. Each "Thinking Hat" entails a different style of thinking:

White Hat: Focus on the data available and analyze it to see what you can learn from it.

Red Hat: Look at the decision using intuition, gut reaction and emotion, and think about how other people will react emotionally.

Black Hat: Look at things pessimistically, cautiously and defensively. Try to see why ideas and approaches might not work.

Yellow Hat: Think positively.

Green Hat: Develop creative solutions to a problem.

Blue Hat: Process control, traffic cop. When chairing meetings, they may direct activity into Green Hat thinking. If contingency plans are needed, they may ask for Black Hat thinking, and so on.

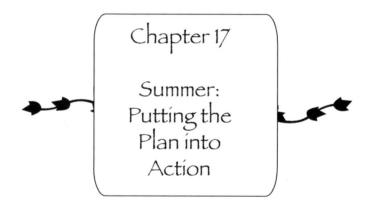

Chapter 17

Summer:
Putting the
Plan into
Action

Summer – Putting the Plan into Action

Summer is the season of carrying out the vision and implementing the plan you have prepared. It is a time of production in critical organizational areas and nourishing that activity, based on the reflection and preparation from the previous seasons. The garden will need plenty of watering: processes, resources and exercises to support and fuel growth. It may also need weeding to overcome and minimize problems that arise.

Intro: Teach the Team to Act

The nurturing leader is sometimes a teacher. This is especially important in this action phase. There are four key strategies for teaching:

- **Excite Them** - build enthusiasm around the purpose.

- **Ground Them** - stewardship, internal audits, breakthrough thinking. Identify issues and failures. Train all levels of the organization.

- **Transform Them** - turn the pyramid into a circle, reward assertiveness, identify coachable moments, choose your battles. Demonstrate how to put insights into practice.

- **Release Them** - turn everyone into a recruiter. Liberate each person's genius. Keep it simple; make them feel comfortable and appreciated.

Managing Change and Growth: PROJECT CHARTER

Project Name: XYZ Pilot Project
Purpose of Project: *The pilot project will be used to accomplish....*
                        The project will also be used to identify barrier to....
Project and Services Background:
Project Goals:
      1.
      2.
Objectives of The Pilot Project:
      1.
      2.
Stakeholders:
Project Constraints:
Risk Management Considerations:
Project Scope: The scope of the project will include the following:
Steering Committee: Membership to include the following
         Representatives:
Steering Committee Deliverables:
Project Sponsors:
Evaluation Process:
Timeline:

Activity:	Target Date:
1.	1.
2.	2.

Management Plan
The three most popular tools for managing projects are work breakdown, critical path, and the Gantt chart.

Work Breakdown
In most cases, it is best to define the end product and then work backwards. A work breakdown analyses all of the discrete tasks and puts them into order for the best workflow. It also shows what tasks must occur before others can start.

Work Breakdown Structure - Setting Up an Office

Setting up an Office

1.0 Project Management	2.0 Design	3.0 Renovate Space	4.0 Technical Services	5.0 Move	6.0 New Office Setup
1.1 Initiated Project	2.1 Analyse Office Function	3.1 Framing	4.1 Prepared Computers & Phones	5.1 Selected & Booked Movers	6.1 Negotiated Lease
1.2 Planned Project	2.2 Develop Work Flow	3.2 Wiring & Plumbing	4.2 Packed Computers & Phones	5.2 Packed Moving Van & Trip	6.2 Unpacked Computers & Phones
1.3 Controlled Project	2.3 Site plan for Work Flow	3.3 Drywall & Finishing		5.3 Unpacked Moving Van	6.3 Installed Computers & Phones
1.4 Closed Project	2.4 Allocate Work locations	3.4 Carpeting			6.4 All other Items Unpacked
		3.5 Decorating			

Adapted from Mount Royal University

Critical Path

After the work tasks have been analyzed, the project can be broken down into key steps. There are usually a number of ways in which they can be ordered. Some tasks must occur in a certain sequence whereas other kinds of tasks may occur simultaneously. A critical path is the sequence of dependent steps that determine the minimum time needed to carry out an operation. In the example below, the critical path is 18 days in length. That means that the product or service must be delivered within that time, if that is the constraint that the total project is under.

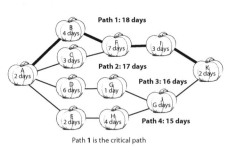

Path 1 is the critical path

Some steps in the workflow are dependent on more than one preceding sequence of steps. In these cases, the minimum time is actually the time needed for the longest preceding sequence.

Progress Plan
To begin, come to agreement on what needs to be accomplished in each of the specific areas with a progress plan.

Progress Notes and Revised Plan of Action

1. Purpose:
2. What Happened:
3. Analysis:
4. Plans:
5. Consultations:
6. Reviews:
7. Termination Report:

Suggestion: Incorporate a regular way of reviewing this information. This will involve deciding what to implement, how to proceed with implementation, and how to evaluate the resulting actions.

Thoughts.....

....

....

....

....

....

....

....

....

Gantt Chart

A Gantt chart shows the tasks and the time they take in a timeline format. It focuses on the deadline dates for each task, resources required and the person responsible.

Here is a sample Action Plan from a collaborative project:

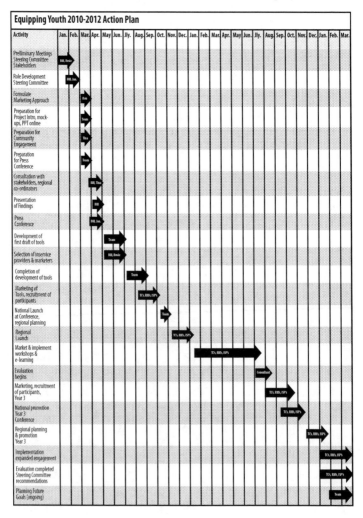

Teaching/coaching/mentoring

There are many tactics and techniques that a leader can draw upon along the way, including workshops, skill development, team building, information sharing and mentoring. In a best-case scenario, they bring about life-changing experiences for all involved, especially the leader(s)! Jones (1996) has many tools in her book, *Teach the Team to Fish.*

As a result of these processes, everyone involved can gain a clearer understanding of vision/mission/goals/objectives, as well as roles and relationship as they relate to their own division and everyday work. It is also an opportunity to develop skills, and leads to a tighter team, improved behaviors (e.g. increased productivity), increased engagement in decision-making, and improved culture.

System Review and Improvement

Along the way, the leader will discover any number of specific systems that need attention. It's not uncommon for organizations to need help with one of the following areas:

- Financial management
- Community inclusion
- Marketing and public awareness
- HR best practices
- Fundraising

Each of these areas requires specialized attention. The depth of detail needed to address every specialized area is beyond the scope of this book. Besides, the leader cannot be an expert in every area and may need to draw on experts on or off the consulting team. However, it is always helpful for an organization when the leader is able to identify areas needing to be attended to, and provides constructive methods to address, monitor and bring accountability to any changes needed. In addition, the leader must play a role in facilitating continuous improvement.

Capacity Assessment – SAMPLE

Each type of system that is going to be improved needs a way of assessing how it has been doing before, during and after the process. The following tool is one example of how to track system improvements.

Systems & Infrastructure	Clear need for increased capacity	Basic level of capacity in place
Planning systems	Planning happens on an ad hoc basis & not supported by collected data	Planning done regularly and some data collected
Decision-making framework	Decisions made primarily on ad hoc basis by one person or whomever available	Appropriate decision-makers known and some kind of decision-making process established but often breaks down
Financial operations management	Gifts and grants deposited and bills paid though not systematic	Transparent financial processes, recorded but could be better tracked
HR management recruiting, training, promotion, rewards	Standard job descriptions unclear, no professional development	Clear job descriptions, some professional development

Adapted from McKinsey & Co.

Fill this in for your organization.

Systems & Infrastructure	Clear need for increased capacity	Basic level of capacity in place
Planning systems		
Decision-making framework		
Financial operations management		
HR management recruiting, training, promotion, rewards		

Capacity Assessment – SAMPLE

Moderate level of capacity in place	High level of capacity in place
Regular planning and some ad hoc planning, some data collected and used systematically	Regular planning & ad hoc planning when needed, formal systems in place to collect & use data
Clearly defined decision-makers and process for decision-making but decisions not well disseminated	Clear, formalized decision-makers and processes, also clearly disseminated
Formal control systems and governance, well-tracked and attention paid to fund flows and cash management	Robust systems and controls in place, all decision-making tracked, cash strategically managed and audited
Clear jobs, professional development, rewards somewhat communicated	Clearly defined jobs, professional development, rewards, promotions and affirmation.

Adapted from McKinsey & Co.

Moderate level of capacity in place	High level of capacity in place

Financial Management – Budget Variances

BUDGET VARIANCE

Approved Budget, Total Year-End Actual Expenditures and Variances

Item	AGENCY	PROJECT			
	1	2	3	4	5
	Approved Budget	Actual Expenditures	Amount of Variance	% of Variance	Explanation
PERSONNEL					
a. Total Personnel	0	0	0	0	0
TRAVEL/PARKING					
b. Total Travel/Parking	0	0	0	0	0
MATERIALS & SUPPLIES					
c. Total Materials & Supplies	0	0	0	0	0
OTHER					
d. Total Other	0	0	0	0	0
e. TOTAL EXPENDITURES	0	0	0	0	0

A common need is some kind of test for evaluating financial management. As usual, it also makes sense to define a check-in process and accountability measures. For example, check for variances between budget and actual expenditures.

Goal Attainment Scale (can also be used as a scoring tool during the fall.)

This tool helps to keep track of progress in an organization, and also aids leadership in setting goals and seeing how those goals are being reached.

Level at intake: * Level at followup: ✔	**Goal Attainment Scale**				
	Goal Headings and Goal Weights				
Check whether or not scale has been mutually negotiated between client and therapist	Yes __ No __	Yes __ No __	Yes __ No __	Yes __ No __	Yes __ No __
Goal Attainment Levels	**Goal 1** **Employment**	**Goal 2** **Protective Order**	**Goal 3** **Housing**	**Goal 4** **Clothing**	**Goal 5** **Day Care**
most unfavorable treatment outcome thought likely (-2)	No applications obtained.	Protective order denied	No housing - no progress toward housing	No progress toward obtaining clothes	No day care
less than expected success with treatment (-1)	Applications obtained.	No progress toward protective order	Waiting list for temporary housing	Vouchers provided, no clothing	Unsatisfactory day care (cost, location, etc)
expected level of treatment success (0)	Applications submitted.	Papers filed for protective order	Temporary or transitional housing	Some clothing obtained	Satisfactory day care obtained
more than expected success with treatment (+1)	Interviews Set.		Transitional housing: list for permanent	Most clothing needs met	Satisfactory day care: list for assistance
best anticipated success with treatment (+2)	Full-time employment obtained	Protective order granted	Permanent housing	All clothing needs met	Satisfactory day care: with financial assistance

Adapted from Thomas Kiresuk

Your Goal Attainment Scale – Fill In

Level at intake: * Level at followup: ✔	**Goal Attainment Scale**				
	Goal Headings and Goal Weights				
Check whether or not scale has been mutually negotiated between client and therapist	Yes __ No __	Yes __ No __	Yes __ No __	Yes __ No __	Yes __ No __
Goal Attainment Levels	**Goal 1**	**Goal 2**	**Goal 3**	**Goal 4**	**Goal 5**
(-2)					
(-1)					
(0)					
(+1)					
(+2)					

Adapted from Thomas Kiresuk

Chapter 18

Fall:
Harvest &
Celebration

Fall: Harvest and Celebration

Fall is a time of harvest – celebration, thanksgiving and counting your blessings. It's the time to collect and enjoy the fruits of everyone's labor. Traditionally, it is also a time for debriefing, giving out rewards and recognition, making public announcements, marketing products, distributing products and rolling out products and services. But fall can also be an opportunity to look at what barriers were encountered in past seasons and how they were dealt with, so that everyone can gain lessons to inform future processes. This is the beginning of a new stage of reflection. In a circle, everyone comes back to the beginning — in this case preparation for next season.

 Take time with your people to enjoy what you have accomplished together and recognize the contributions of everyone.

But be sure to also take time to evaluate the degree to which leadership has been effective and the capacity building process have been successful.

Outcomes and Evaluation
It can be helpful to provide some kind of quantifiable measurement to the process of evaluation.

* *Goal Attainment Scale* This tool was used in Summer to establish goals, and now can be used to compare actual results to expected results. Then tabulate the score.

* *Logic Model* In the same fashion, this tool was used in Spring to define expected outcomes, and can now be used to compare actual outcomes to expected outcomes.

In the Fall, the harvested fruits are linked to what was planted in the Spring. It is important that everyone sees how the planting and watering that occurred in the Spring came into fruition in the Summer and matured in the Fall. It is a way of marking the seasons, and one great tactic to do this is focus groups. It is best to bring in an outside consultant to moderate, so that everyone can participate freely.

How to Conduct a Focus Group

Before the session:
1. *Define the objectives.* Identify end goals and ensure a focus group is the appropriate way to meet these objectives.

2. *Choose a moderator.* Be sure the moderator is skilled in facilitating discussion; he/she should be a good listener who understands the intent of the study and can give all participants a chance to voice their opinions. They should also prevent any participants from dominating discussion and influencing the opinions of others.

3. *Prepare eight to twelve questions that generate continuous conversation.* Arrange the questions into a sequence that is appropriate to the objectives, and prepare some follow-up questions that will prompt respondents to elaborate on their answers.

4. *Test the questions before finalizing them.* They should provide enough information without inspiring tedious discussions. Experience dictates that these questions be tested with colleagues, the project Consultant committee, or other project stakeholders.

5. *Recruit participants.* Carefully consider the background and experiences of prospective participants, and establish qualification criteria for selection.

6. *Offer incentives* to participants such as refreshments, childcare, and/or monetary compensation.

7. *Have participants sign consent forms.* Participants must be fully informed about the purpose of your focus group and what you will do with the information they provide. Written consent should be obtained whenever possible.

8. *Find an appropriate space* such as a conference room or private office.

9. *Develop an outline of questions and topics to guide the discussion.* Make sure it is easy for the moderator to follow and indicate how much time should be spent on each topic area.

10. *Set up recording equipment.* Focus groups are usually videotaped or audio taped. Ask for participants' permission ahead of time.

11. *Assign a note taker.* Have someone on the research team take notes to support the video/audio recordings. If taking notes is the only way of recording sessions, make sure the note taker is prepared to take thorough notes.

During the session:

1. *Explain the purpose.* "Why is this focus group being conducted?"

2. *Explain how you will record the discussion and use the results.* "Who will see or hear the conversation or its results?" Participants will want assurance that confidentiality will be respected.

3. *Use an exercise to warm-up the group.* Pass out nametags and play a name game or other warm-up exercise.

4. *Move from general to specific topics.* Begin with the most general questions to get people talking, then move on to more detailed, specific questions.

5. *Be creative.* Periodic short exercises will help maintain interest and engagement.

6. *Finish the session* by reviewing the key ideas and ask for confirmation or additional thoughts.

After the session:

1. *Summarize data collected.* Reserve time between sessions to summarize what has been learned.
2. *Transcribe your data.* Type out all dialogue. If possible, have an experienced transcriber take on this position to save time.
3. *Be prepared to analyze your data.* Learn about qualitative data analysis (e.g. coding, categorizing, comparing, and contrasting responses). See below for resources on qualitative analysis.
4. *Be careful in generalizing your findings for a larger population.* Because these findings are based on a small group, they are more suitable for exploring new research questions or topics, or explaining or confirming previous findings.
5. *Prepare a report.* Address the focus group questions and use quotes for illustration. Have a section for conclusions and suggest next steps.

Checklist for Planning and Benefiting from a Focus Group:

- *Have clear objectives been established for conducting a focus group?*
- *Has a skilled moderator been selected?*
- *Have clear selection criteria been determined for selection of participants?*
- *Have focus group questions and a discussion outline been prepared?*
- *Has recording equipment been arranged & tested? Insightful quotes recorded?*
- *Will the consultant (& team) analyze qualitative data & discuss the results?*
- *Have quotes, conclusions & suggestions all been included in the report?*

Time to Contemplate

If possible, develop a schedule that permits whatever processes are needed to appraise completion of a project - individual evaluation (to all staff involved with the project), group discussion related to the project, and expert witness. Meta-analysis stands back from the entire project and allows the evaluation to sink in, asking key questions - What was the purpose of the project? Did the knowledge and skills match everyone's roles and responsibilities? How were they evaluated? Who made the decisions and how were they made? Look at the ability of the leaders and managers to lead and manage. What about succession? The consultant needs to help everyone define the objective, interlinking and providing connections across the organization with the leader - and his Board. Also involve recipients of service in surveys - what did they get out of the renewed programs and services? What recommendations would they have for the future?

Performance Appraisal

```
Objectives: _____

          _____

What happened: _____

          _____
```

Many organizations conduct their performance appraisals at this time, once the dust has settled.

Communication

Always stay in touch - share lessons learned, by broadcast e-mail or town hall meetings. A town hall meeting PPT might include: welcome, reiteration of project activities (types and numbers of meetings, processes and events), summary of outcomes, summary of findings and recommendations, discussion questions that arose from the process, what was learned. Compile ideas of how to go forward and make good on decisions to date.

How can you do this in your division?

_____

_____

_____

_____

Celebration

Remember to have fun - help everyone enjoy the fruits of each other's labour - recognizing achievements of individuals and departments with staff rewards and certificates. Consider asking recipients of the programs and services to give their testimonies and acknowledge how the work of the organization has ultimately made a difference.

When is this the best time to do this in your division?

_____

_____

_____

_____

_____

_____

Chapter 19

Next:
New Season

Next: Back to Winter

Take the lessons learned and use them to prepare for next season (the next phase of organizational development). Renegotiate relationships or graduate the gardener. Facilitate ongoing organizational learning and continuous improvement.

Winter

It's time to start over - Winter is coming. As you head back into a time of reflection and light, enjoy the fruits of the harvest while planning and thinking about how to improve it for next year.

Reflection and evaluation

In summary, this is the best time for the nurturing leader to find out where they thought their organization would be, to tabulate lessons learned, to perform reporting and to digest the lessons for next season. Tools: Project evaluation tools, sample evaluations and reports. It's a time to stand back, look at the garden, use the fruits and plan what you would change for the future.

Epilogue

This book is a living document. We are learning as we go and invite you to participate in the ongoing process related to this project.

Let us know how *The Nurturing Leader* has impacted you, what parts you found most helpful, and any stories you have about how it has been used.

Contact us:

bill@capacitybuilders.org
www.capacitybuilders.org

Bibliography

Christie, J. (1988). Fiscal crisis and the threat of strategic change in a human service organization: A case study of the impact of managerial decisions in a community living project for the severely mentally and physically disabled. Ph.D. dissertation, University of Alberta (Canada), Canada. Retrieved May 27, 2020, from Dissertations & Theses: Full Text. (Publication No. AAT NL42761).

De Bono, E. (2010). *Six thinking hats.* London, UK: Penguin Books (UK)

Dent, F.N. (2003). *The leadership pocketbook.* London, UK: Management Pocketbooks.

Hicks, E. & Hicks, J. (2006). *Law of attraction: The basics of the teachings of abraham.* Carlsbad, CA: Hay House.

Ingham, H. & Luft, J. (1955). The Johari Window, A Graphic Model of Interpersonal Awareness. *Proceedings of the Western Training Laboratory in Group Development.* Los Angeles: University of California, Los Angeles.

Jones, L. (1996). *Jesus, CEO: Using ancient wisdom for visionary leadership.* New York, NY: Hyperion Books.

Kiresuk, T. (1994). *Brief history of goal attainment scaling.* East Sussex, UK: Psychology Press.

McKinsey & Co. (2001). *Effective capacity building in nonprofit organizations.* Washington, DC: Venture Philanthropy Partners.

Miller, S. & Duncan, B. (1996). *The outcome and session rating scales: Administration and scoring manual.* Chicago, IL: Institute for the Study of Therapeutic Change.

Morgan, G. (1997). *Imaginization: New mindsets of seeing, organizing and managing.* San Francisco, CA: Berrett-Koehler Publishers.

Mount Royal University. (2007). *Work Breakdown Structure.* Calgary, AB: Project Management Dept.

Ross, K. (1969). *On death and dying.* London, UK: Tavistock/Routledge.

Senge, P. (2006). *The fifth discipline: The art and practice of the learning organization.* New York, NY: Doubleday, a division of Random House Inc.

Sobel, A. & Sheth, J. (2002). *Clients for life: Evolving from an expert-for-hire to an extraordinary adviser.* New York, NY: Free Press/Simon & Schuster.

Tichy, N. (1983). *Managing strategic change: Technical, political, and cultural dynamics (Wiley Series on Organizational Assessment and Change).* Hoboken, NJ: John Wiley and Sons.

Appendix: Other Resources and Tools

Overview: The past few decades have seen an explosion in the number of useful tools to help change agents effectively explore, understand and communicate about organizations, as well as to consult successful change in those organizations.

The following is a list of additional tools and where to find them, including exercises, questionnaires, checklists, dynamic instruments, analysis tools and templates. There are also interactive and qualitative methods.

- Books
- Consultants
- Articles
- Websites
- People
- Associations
- Events

Compendium: "Capacity Builders: Library and Online Resources.doc"

Consulting and Capacity Building

http://www.capacitybuilders.org/
http://www.acf.hhs.gov/programs/ccf/about_ccf/promising_
practices/content.html
http://www.authenticityconsulting.com/pubs/CN-gdes/CN-pubs.
htm#anchor12535

"The Capacity Building Challenge; PART I: A Research Perspective, PART II: A Funder's Response.pdf" (Foundation Centre)

"Promising Practices for Improving the Capacity of Faith- and Community-Based Organizations"

Million Dollar Consulting and "Million Dollar Consulting Toolkit.pdf's" by Alan Weiss

Clients for Life by Sheth and Sobel

First Things First by Stephen Covey

"Guidelines on the Use of Consultants.pdf" (Asian Development Bank)

"Handbook for users of consulting services.doc"(Asian Development Bank)

Common Types of Capacity Building
(from: "Field Consultant to Consulting and Organizational Development With Nonprofits")

Building Capacity in Nonprofit Organizations.pdf, Urban Institute Press
Qualitative Study of the Challenges Facing Canada's Nonprofits and Voluntary Sector – Cdn Centre for Phil 2003

Making Nonprofits Work: A Report on the Tides of Nonprofit Management Reform by Paul Light – Brookings Institution Press

Funding Effectiveness: Lessons in Building Nonprofit Capacity by Barbara Kibbe (in Grantmakers for Effective Organizations) http://www.geofunders.org/

Capacity Building: Beware the Easy Fix, order from Nonprofit Quarterly

Capacity Building for Impact: The Future of Effectiveness for Nonprofits and Foundations

Echoes from the Field: Proven Capacity Building Principles for Nonprofits

Effective Capacity Building in Nonprofit Organizations

How to "Do" Capacity Building (Council on Foundations)

Lessons from the Street: Capacity Building and Replication

Mapping Nonprofit Capacity Builders: A Study by LaSalle University's Nonprofit Center

Nonprofit Capacity Building Toolkit, order from Authenticity Consulting, LLC

Reflections on Capacity Building by California Wellness Center (online).

Results of an Inquiry into Capacity Building Programs for Nonprofits

Strengthening Nonprofit Organizations: A Funder's Consultant to Capacity Building

Non-Profit and Community Organizations
http://www.managementhelp.org/org_perf/capacity.htm
http://www.charityvillage.com/cv/research/index.asp (org dev't portal)
http://www.fieldstonealliance.org/client/client_images/pdfs/
Fieldstone_Alliance_Spring_2008_Book_Catalog.pdf
http://www.afpnet.org/resource_center
http://www.cra-arc.gc.ca/tax/charities/menu-e.html
http://www.charityvillage.ca/cv/main.asp
http://www.charitychannel.com
http://www.rcvo.org/bookadinclude/bookorderform.pdf
http://www.nonprofitscan.ca/
http://www.boarddevelopment.org/display_document.
cfm?document_id=69
http://www.boarddevelopment.org/
http://www.iog.ca/
http://www.nonprofitquarterly.org/
http://nonprofitscan.imaginecanada.ca/en/browse_by_subject
http://tamarackcommunity.ca/index.php
http://www.managementhelp.org/emp_well/spirit.htm
http://www.wildrosefoundation.ca/partnershipkit/default.aspx

http://books.google.ca/books?id=RhoACTugjk4C&dq=Governing
+for+Results:+A+Director%27s+Consultant+to+Good+Governan
ce&pg=PP1&ots=958hCdxAzT&sig=6tRVfznc-
http://rcvo.andornot.com/Library/LibrarySearch.aspx
http://www.mncn.org/index.htm
http://www.boarddevelopment.org/

Governing for Results by Mel Gill

Building an Effective Board of Directors (Association of
Fundraising Professionals)

"Consultant for Boards.pdf" (Industry Canada)

Tools – Consulting, Business, Legal, etc.
http://www.charityvillage.com/cv/research/index.asp (org dev't
portal)
http://www.innonet.org/ (org dev't portal)
http://www.adb.org/Consulting/documents.asp
http://www.businessballs.com/
http://www.acf.hhs.gov/programs/ccf/resources/toolkit.html
http://www.evaluationtools.org/tools_main.asp
http://www.coco-net.org/resources.html
http://www.uslegalforms.com/
http://www.unitedway.org/outcomes/
http://www.acf.hhs.gov/programs/ccf/resources/toolkit.html
http://www.arcco.ca/html/resources.html
http://plot.bclibrary.ca/about/memorandum-of-understanding
http://www.hrcouncil.ca/tools/pg001_e.cfm
http://www.innonet.org/index.php?section_id=64&content_id=185
http://www.hrsg.ca/
http://www.templatezone.com/index.php
http://www.fieldstonealliance.org/client/client_pages/tools.
cfm#assessment
http://contracts.onecle.com/type/4.shtml
http://www.asaecenter.org/PublicationsResources/modelcatlist.
cfm?navItemNumber=16061
http://www.law-nonprofit.org/links.htm

http://www.wildrosefoundation.ca/partnershipkit/default.aspx
http://www.afpnet.org/resource_center
http://nicholasf.wordpress.com/2008/07/09/what-is-a-
partnership-agreement/
http://www.wkkf.org/Pubs/CustomPubs/CPtoolkit/cptoolkit/
Sec3-menu.htm
http://www.bnet.com/2405-13055_23-41874.html

"Field "Effective Capacity Building FULL REPORT.pdf"
by McKinsey & Co.

"Capacity Building - Lessons Learned.pdf" Venture
Philanthropy Partners - by McKinsey & Co.

The Consultant's Big Book of Organization Development Tools
: 50 Reproducible Intervention Tools to Help Solve Your Clients'
Problems
by Mel Silberman

The Consultant's Toolkit: High-Impact Questionnaires,
Activities and How-to Consultants for Diagnosing and Solving
Client Problems (Paperback)
by Mel Silberman

"Consultant to Consulting and Organizational Development
With Nonprofits.pdf"

"Million Dollar Consulting Toolkit.pdf" by Alan Weiss

"Capacity Assessment Grid.pdf' by McKinsey & Co.

"Why Do Evaluation?" by Michael Wells http://www.
charitychannel.com

"The Non-Profit Organization Self-Evaluation Checklist.pdf" by
Ginsler and Associates Inc

"A Developmental Evaluation Primer.pdf" published by JW
McConnell Family Foundation

Workshop Ideas, etc.
http://www.businessballs.com/
http://sf2.strengthsfinder.com/
http://www.chapters.indigo.ca/books/Now-Discover-
Your-Strengths-Marcus-Buckingham-Donald-O-
Clifton/9780743201148-item.html
http://community.tisch.nyu.edu/page/workshop.html

"Service Canada Community Capacity Building Facilitators
Handbook" (Service Canada)

**Organizational Theory –Change Management and
Community Development, etc.**
http://www.managementhelp.org/org_chng/org_chng.htm
http://www.muttart.org/publications.htm
http://en.outreach.ca/WhatWeDo/ChurchHealthRevitalization/
VisionRenewal/Ove
http://www.volunteercalgary.ab.ca/resources/res_books.html
http://www.theoryofchange.org/
http://www.servicelearning.org/resources/index.php
http://www.dvc.vic.gov.au/web14/dvc/dvcmain.nsf/
headingpagesdisplay/building+stronger+communities
http://www.communityplanning.net/index.htm
http://www.asaecenter.org/PublicationsResources/
http://www.hrcouncil.ca/index_e.cfm
http://www.axi.ca/
http://sec.oise.utoronto.ca/english/workshops.php
http://www.coveyperformance.com/
http://www.coco-net.org/resources.html
http://rcvo.andornot.com/Library/LibrarySearch.aspx
http://www.conferenceboard.ca/Default.htm
http://www.mncn.org/index.htm

Forces for Good: The Six Practises of High-Impact Nonprofits
by Leslie R. Crutchfield and Heather McLeod Grant

Policy

http://www.nvit.ca/institutionalpolicies/boardgovernance/
a.2.1.1summary.html
http://www.iog.ca/policity/CP/index.html

Guide to Writing Bylaws by Mel Gill

About the Authors

Bill Locke, M.E.F.M.

Bill Locke is the President of Capacity Builders, a consulting company focused on the development of leaders and organizations in the charitable sector. He and his staff have worked with over 200 non-profit organizations around the world, including faith-based organizations, non-profit agencies, foundations and government departments.

From 1986 to 1996, Locke served as Founding Executive Director of Cornerstone Communications, a charitable organization providing training and professional services to nonprofits across Canada. Cornerstone pioneered the use of social enterprise in the area of marketing and communications for other charities, developing strategic plans, creating advertising campaigns, and performing fundraising and recruitment.

Locke has also written and produced educational videos, documentaries, and television programs. These have covered a wide variety of topics, including gambling addiction, student debt, adoption, alternative medicine and spiritual growth.

Joel Christie, PhD

Dr. Joel Christie is currently a Social Planner for FCSS in Calgary. His portfolio includes the seniors sector as well as InformCalgary.

Dr. Christie has over 40 years of direct senior and executive management experience and specializes in the development of organizations and the management of strategic change in human service organizations. His Masters degree specialized in Community Development and his doctoral studies focused on Organization Development and the Management of Strategic Change in complex organizations focusing especially on the Health system.

Dr. Christie has worked directly with and made presentations to private, voluntary and government sectors at international, provincial and community levels. These undertakings have included facilitating projects on visioning, strategic management, program planning, staff development and personal coaching. He has also worked with persons and organizations in both the private and public sectors to help them re-examine their mission and revitalize their sense of commitment to the mission and markets.